THE BEDFORD SERIES IN HISTORY AND CULTURE

The Chinese Exclusion Act and Angel Island
A Brief History with Documents

Judy Yung

University of California, Santa Cruz

bedford/st.martin's
Macmillan Learning
Boston | New York

For Bedford/St. Martin's

Vice President, Editorial, Macmillan Learning Humanities: Edwin Hill
Senior Program Director for History: Michael Rosenberg
Senior Program Manager for History: William J. Lombardo
History Marketing Manager: Melissa Rodriguez
Director of Content Development, Humanities: Jane Knetzger
Developmental Editor: Mary P. Starowicz
Content Project Manager: Lidia MacDonald-Carr
Senior Workflow Project Manager: Lisa McDowell
Production Supervisor: Robert Cherry
Senior Media Project Manager: Michelle Camisa
Manager of Publishing Services: Andrea Cava
Project Management: Lumina Datamatics, Inc.
Composition: Lumina Datamatics, Inc.
Permissions Manager: Kalina Ingham
Permission Associate: Michael McCarty
Text Permission Researcher: Arthur Johnson, Lumina Datamatics, Inc.
Director of Rights and Permissions: Hilary Newman
Director of Design, Content Management: Diana Blume
Cover Design: Willam Boardman
Cover Art: (front cover) Courtesy National Archives, Washington, D.C.; (back cover)
  © Jim MacKenzie
Printing and Binding: LSC Communications

Manufactured in the United States of America.

2 3 4 5 6 7   22 21 20 19 18

For information, write: Bedford/St. Martin's, 75 Arlington Street, Boston, MA 02116

ISBN 978-1-319-07786-0

Acknowledgments
Text acknowledgments and copyrights appear at the back of the book on pages 167–68, which constitute an extension of the copyright page. Art acknowledgments and copyrights appear on the same page as the art selections they cover.

In memory of my brother Warren Tom Yung (1948–2017),

Chinese American historian Philip P. Choy (1926–2017),

and

my loving husband Eddie Fung (1922–2018)

Foreword

The Bedford Series in History and Culture is designed so that readers can study the past as historians do.

The historian's first task is finding the evidence. Documents, letters, memoirs, interviews, pictures, movies, novels, or poems can provide facts and clues. Then the historian questions and compares the sources. There is more to do than in a courtroom, for hearsay evidence is welcome, and the historian is usually looking for answers beyond act and motive. Different views of an event may be as important as a single verdict. How a story is told may yield as much information as what it says.

Along the way the historian seeks help from other historians and perhaps from specialists in other disciplines. Finally, it is time to write, to decide on an interpretation and how to arrange the evidence for readers.

Each book in this series contains an important historical document or group of documents, each document a witness from the past and open to interpretation in different ways. The documents are combined with some element of historical narrative—an introduction or a biographical essay, for example—that provides students with an analysis of the primary source material and important background information about the world in which it was produced.

Each book in the series focuses on a specific topic within a specific historical period. Each provides a basis for lively thought and discussion about several aspects of the topic and the historian's role. Each is short enough (and inexpensive enough) to be a reasonable one-week assignment in a college course. Whether as classroom or personal reading, each book in the series provides firsthand experience of the challenge—and fun—of discovering, recreating, and interpreting the past.

Lynn Hunt
David W. Blight
Bonnie G. Smith

Preface

The fifth daughter of immigrant parents from China, I grew up in the 1950s knowing very little about my own family history, let alone Chinese American history, which was never mentioned in any of the public schools I attended. Like everyone else in San Francisco Chinatown, my family went by two different surnames. Among our relatives and friends, we were known as the Tom family, but at school and on our birth certificates, we were known as the Yung family. We always knew that if ever questioned by the "foreign devils," we were not to reveal our real Chinese surname; otherwise, the family would be in big trouble. I never understood why until I found out about a place called Angel Island in 1975.

Word had been going around Chinatown that a park ranger named Alexander Weiss had seen Chinese poems carved into the walls of an old immigration building on Angel Island in San Francisco Bay. That piqued my interest, and I made a trip there to see for myself. A ranger led a group of us to a two-story wooden barracks, some of its windows boarded over, behind a barbed wire fence. The first-floor dormitory was empty except for twenty-eight standing poles from which three tiers of beds had once hung. Sunlight streamed through dirty windows onto the littered floor and the peeling walls covered with verse. With the aid of a flashlight, I could make out Chinese calligraphy—line after line of poetry in the classical style that had been brushed and etched into the wood. Touching the chipped paint that covered the words, I could hear the immigrants' voices. "Grief and bitterness entwined are heaven sent," one wrote. "Sadness kills the person in the wooden building," wrote another. Moved to tears, I wondered why I had never heard of this place.

Soon after my visit, I asked my father if he knew about Angel Island. At first he brushed me off, but finally he said, "Yeah, that's where they kept us when we first arrived." I later learned that in order to circumvent the Chinese Exclusion Act, which prohibited the immigration of Chinese laborers, my father Tom Yip Jing came to this country claiming to be Yung Hin Sen, the seventeen-year-old son of a Chinese merchant in Stockton, California. Detained on Angel Island for thirty-four days, he was grilled about his family background, village life, and whatever he knew about his father's life in America. When the immigrant inspector found no discrepancies in his answers when compared to those of his father and brother, he was believed to be the son of Yung Dung and duly admitted into the country. Like my father, the overwhelming majority of Chinese immigrants who came during the exclusion period (1882–1943) were "paper sons" of merchants or U.S. citizens. They took this "crooked path" because that was the only way they could come. The price they paid was heavy. Many were forced to live a life of deceit and duplicity, under constant fear of detection and deportation, until the day they died. It was a well-kept secret, as was the harsh treatment accorded them at the immigration station. No wonder that they never wanted to tell their children about this cursed place—Angel Island.

Until recently, U.S. immigration history, as taught in classrooms across the country, has usually centered on the celebratory story of the 12 million European immigrants who came through Ellis Island and went on to realize their American dreams while contributing to the building of this great nation. Missing from this history lesson has been the tragic story of Chinese exclusion and the ordeal of detention at Angel Island, the "Ellis Island of the West," for the 100,000 Chinese immigrants who came across the Pacific seeking the same American dream. This book will introduce students to a fuller, more complex, and diverse picture of U.S. immigration history; provide them with the tools to participate in the current debates on immigration, race, and national identity; and teach them how historians do research using primary documents, oral histories, and poetry as historical evidence in their work.

What is uniquely important about this book are the personal stories and viewpoints of proponents and opponents of the Chinese exclusion laws; of Chinese immigrants who posed as "paper sons" and "paper daughters" to evade the exclusion laws; and of immigration officials who held strong convictions about how the immigration laws should be enforced. The book opens with a comprehensive yet concise introduction to the history of Chinese immigration, the anti-Chinese movement and public debate over the Chinese Exclusion Act, the enforcement of the exclusion laws at Angel Island, and the impact of Chinese exclusion on Chinese Americans, U.S. immigration policy, and our understanding of what it means to be an American—then and now. The introduction in Part One provides students with an overarching historical, socioeconomic, and political context by which to understand the compilation of primary documents that follow. For the same reason, each document has its own headnote with background information about the author and comments on its historical significance.

The primary documents in Part Two are broken into four thematic categories. The first, "The Road to Exclusion," covers the diverse perspectives of organized labor, politicians, and the Chinese community in the public debate surrounding Chinese immigration. They are drawn from newspaper accounts, memorials, and government documents like the *Congressional Record*. Together, they reveal the racial biases Americans used to define who can be an American, as well as the arguments and strategies that the Chinese community and their allies used in their fight against racial exclusion.

The next section, "Representations of the Chinese in the Popular Press," includes literary and pictorial documents that perpetrated stereotypes of the Chinese as cheap labor, heathens, and wily tricksters unfit for citizenship and a threat to American society. Reflections as well as molders of public opinion, these images abounded in the popular press of the day as political commentary and as justification for Chinese exclusion.

"Enforcing the Chinese Exclusion Laws" examines the immigration process from the vantage points of the excluder and the excluded through immigration documents found at the National Archives, Chinese and English-language journals and newspapers, privately published position papers, oral history interviews that were conducted in the 1970s, and Chinese poetry. The official correspondence and reports of local and federal immigration officials will help students understand the motivation and rationale behind their policies, practices, and decisions, while the oral history interviews with an immigrant inspector, an interpreter, and two Chinese detainees will provide students with an insider's perspective on the ordeal of detention at Angel Island. Most poignant and haunting are the translations of some of the Chinese poems that were found carved into the barrack walls of the detention building.

The document selections end with "Correcting a Historic Mistake," which covers the reasons for the repeal of the Chinese Exclusion Acts in 1943 and congressional regrets in 2011. This section makes the important connections between the past and present debate on immigration policies and reform. Students are asked to ponder the questions: "Have we learned from the mistakes of our past?" and "How can we best fix the broken immigration system while remaining true to our values as a nation of immigrants with liberty and justice for all?"

The appendix material—Chronology, Questions for Consideration, and Bibliography—will help students see the larger picture and critical junctures in U.S. immigration history; generate classroom discussions on a variety of immigration issues; and guide them in their own research, analysis, and writing assignments.

Students in U.S. history and Asian American studies classes will appreciate this book's definitive introduction on Chinese immigration and exclusion, the rich array of primary documents from multiple perspectives, and its highly readable narrative style of writing. *Chinese Exclusion and Angel Island* promises to introduce students to a broader and more inclusive vision of U.S. immigration history and, ultimately, a better understanding of the world we live in.

A NOTE ON THE TEXT

Following standard practice, when using a person's Chinese name, I give the surname (family name) first, followed by the given name (usually two characters). For example, in the name Ng Poon Chew, Ng is the surname and Poon Chew, the given name. I use the Hanyu Pinyin system for Chinese proper names, except in cases where the names have been commonly spelled in a different Romanization system. For common words and phrases in the Cantonese dialect or direct quotes from Cantonese-speaking persons, I use the Cantonese spelling.

No attempt has been made to correct spellings, punctuation, or grammar in the primary documents in order to remain faithful to the exact wording and style of speech. Outdated and derogatory terms like "Chinaman," "Oriental," or "coolie" appear in the book as part of the historical record from which they were drawn and reflect the perspective of the times.

ACKNOWLEDGMENTS

Chinese Exclusion and Angel Island is an accumulation of forty years of research by leading scholars and colleagues Him Mark Lai, Philip P. Choy, and Erika Lee. I am grateful to them for building the foundation upon which this book rests and for their generosity in sharing their research findings and archival collections with me. I am also grateful to the resourceful librarians and archivists at the University of California, Santa Cruz, and the National Archives in San Bruno, California, for their research assistance; to Gisela R. Ables, Angela Hawk, Erika Lee, Franklin Ng, John Kuo-Wei Tchen, Seneca Vaught, and R. Scott Wong for their critical feedback on the first draft; to Marlon Hom for his exact translations; to Vincent Chin for his scanning skills; and to Grant Din, Eddie Fung, and Ruthanne Lum McCunn for their unflagging support. Thank you to the team at Bedford/St. Martin's that made this possible: Program Director Michael Rosenberg, History Marketing Manager Melissa Rodriguez, Content Project Manager Lidia MacDonald-Carr, Cover Designer William Boardman, and to Senior Program Manager William Lombardo and Development Editor Mary P. Starowicz, for their patience and editorial guidance.

Judy Yung

Contents

Illustrations

Illustrations

PART ONE

Introduction:
Chinese Immigration
to the United States

On May 6, 1882, Congress and President Chester Arthur changed the course of U.S. history by passing and signing the Chinese Exclusion Act into law. The new law suspended for ten years the entry of Chinese laborers into the United States; set policies for admitting, tracking, and deporting Chinese immigrants unlawfully in the country; and forbade state and federal courts from granting Chinese residents U.S. citizenship. It marked the first time in U.S. history that lawmakers closed America's gates to a specific immigrant group based on race, nationality, and class. Calling it a "historic mistake," President Franklin D. Roosevelt successfully pushed for the act's repeal in 1943; however, the official racism it sanctioned was not removed from U.S. immigration policy until President Lyndon B. Johnson signed the Immigration and Nationality Act of 1965 into law.

The Chinese Exclusion Act marked the end of free immigration to the United States and the beginning of restricted immigration and racial exclusion. In subsequent years, additional laws were passed to bar other Asian groups and to limit immigration from Southern and Eastern European countries based on eugenicist notions of preserving the "Nordic race." Why were the Chinese the first to be singled out for exclusion? What were the social, economic, and political causes behind their exclusion? How were the exclusion laws enforced, particularly at the Angel

1

Island Immigration Station, the primary point of entry for Chinese immigrants between 1910 and 1940? How did the Chinese resist what they termed "laws harsh as tigers" and redress their grievances? And what were the long-term impacts and legacies of Chinese exclusion on generations of Chinese Americans, U.S. immigration policies, and our understanding of what it means to be an American then and now?

ORIGINS OF CHINESE IMMIGRATION

The roots of Chinese immigration to the United States extend back to the 1500s and the era of European colonization, when competing empires expanded into Asia in search of wealth, trade, and cheap labor to work in their newly developing economies. The Spanish Empire was the first to establish trade between Asia and the Americas in 1565, which resulted in its ships bringing some 100,000 Asian sailors, slaves, and servants from the Philippines to Acapulco in New Spain (present-day Mexico). The continued expansion of European empires, and the subsequent rise of the British Empire in the Indian subcontinent and China, led to the recruitment of indentured workers to fill a labor shortage in the Caribbean and South America created by the end of British trade in African slaves in 1807. The United States also turned to China in the mid-nineteenth century for sought-after Chinese goods and for laborers needed to develop the American West.[1]

The first wave of Chinese to immigrate to the United States came principally from the Pearl River Delta of Guangdong Province in southeastern China. Attracted by stories of the Gold Rush in California, they came not only as miner-prospectors but also as artisans, professionals, merchants, and students. From 1852 until 1882, when the Chinese Exclusion Act was passed, more than 300,000 Chinese entered the United States. They helped fuel the expansion of American capitalism by providing a continuous stream of labor to drive its burgeoning industries and profits.

It is no accident that the Chinese were chosen to play this important role in America's development. U.S. interest in China first began after the Revolutionary War, when the new republic was cut off from trading within the British commonwealth. In 1784, the *Empress of China* sailed from New York to Canton laden with furs, lead, wine, Mexican silver dollars, and American ginseng. It returned a year later with a ship full of porcelain, tea, and silk, making a large profit for its investors. For a long time, officials of the Qing dynasty (1644–1911) had resisted opening ports to European traders, who sought China's treasures but had little to offer in return. China restricted foreign commerce to the port of Canton and required that all business be conducted through the *cohong*, a licensed group of merchants.

Great Britain led the Western powers in forcing China to open to trade. Looking for a way to tip the trade imbalance that was in China's favor, the British began smuggling Indian-grown opium into the country in 1820. Alarmed by the severe addiction problem created by the smuggling, the Chinese government took action in 1839 by sending Commissioner Lin Zexu to Canton, where he promptly destroyed more than 20,000 chests of British opium before closing the port to trade. This sparked the first Opium War (1839–1842), in which the British navy easily defeated the poorly trained and equipped imperial forces. Under the Treaty of Nanking, China was forced to cede Hong Kong to the British, open five ports to foreign commerce, pay an indemnity of 21 million silver dollars, and grant Britain and its allies extraterritorial rights, which in essence made them immune to Chinese law. A second Opium War (1856–1860) with Britain and France wrested further concessions from the Chinese. In 1868, the United States signed a separate treaty with China known as the Burlingame Treaty, which guaranteed the free flow of trade and immigration between the two countries.[2]

These treaties had an adverse, trickle-down effect on the common people in the southeastern province of Guangdong. Porters and dockhands became unemployed as the port of Canton lost its monopoly on trade. Domestic industries could not compete with imported manufactured goods. The opium trade drove up the price of silver, which was the standard for payment of taxes, and increased taxes to pay war indemnities led to the forfeiture of land, unemployment, and poverty. To make matters worse, Chinese peasants also had to contend with overpopulation and the shortage of arable land, periodic droughts and floods, and the devastation caused by inter ethnic feuds and the Taiping Rebellion against the Qing dynasty. Emigration, despite an imperial ban on pain of death since 1728, became a desperate option.

Many Chinese in the Pearl River Delta of Guangdong, because of their coastal location and early contact with foreign traders, were lured to the Americas by promises of high wages from labor recruiters and by stories of the Gold Rush in California. Some 250,000 Chinese men were abducted, tricked, and forced to work as indentured laborers in the sugar plantations and guano mines of the West Indies, Cuba, and Peru as part of the notorious coolie trade (1847–1874). In contrast to these *unfree* laborers who were legally bound by contract, another

300,000 Chinese sailed from Hong Kong to the United States between 1852 and 1882 as *free* laborers. They either paid their own way or used the credit-ticket system, in which they borrowed money from a broker and later paid it back with interest from their earnings. Despite this distinction, public opinion often mischaracterized the importation of Chinese laborers as "coolies"—a new system of slavery that degraded American labor.[3] By the latter part of the nineteenth century, emigration patterns had been firmly established, and many villages in the Pearl River Delta came to depend on the remittances sent by their men working overseas.

The overwhelming majority of Chinese immigrants to the United States were young men who intended to strike it rich and return home. Chinese prospectors, coming from a greater distance across the Pacific, were among the last to arrive for the Gold Rush. At least half of them were married, but most did not bring their wives and families. Because of cultural mores that dictated that women remain at home and the harsh living conditions in the American West, it was cheaper and safer for the men to maintain a split household and support their families in China from across the seas. After 1875, U.S. immigration laws made it more difficult for Chinese women to join their husbands in America. So few Chinese women immigrated that throughout the nineteenth century, they never exceeded 5 percent of the Chinese population in the United States. This absence of women set the patterns of Chinese immigration, employment, and community development apart from those of most other immigrant groups, resulting in a mobile labor force and a bachelor society marred by social vices—gambling, drugs, prostitution, and tong (gang) wars.[4] The Chinese population, virtually all adult males, made a greater impact on the economy than their numbers would indicate. In 1870, they constituted 8 percent of California's population but one quarter of the state's labor force.

As the United States expanded westward occupying new lands taken from Mexico and Native Americans, industrialization and the growth of American capitalism created an insatiable need for labor to extract natural resources, build a transportation infrastructure, and clear land for cultivation. Many of these jobs were deemed dirty, dangerous, and undesirable by white workers, but Chinese desperate to make a living accepted the work despite being paid even less. Beginning in 1864, some 12,000 Chinese, representing 90 percent of Central Pacific Railroad's entire work force, were recruited from San Francisco and Hong Kong to help build the western end of the transcontinental railroad. Despite their small physical stature, the Chinese worked in all phases of construction—leveling roadbeds, boring tunnels, blasting mountainsides, and laying tracks. Many died in explosive accidents or were buried in snow avalanches while digging tunnels through the Sierra Nevada mountains during the winter months. As railroad baron Leland Stanford acknowledged, "Without them it would be impossible to complete the western portion of this great national Highway."[5]

Having proven their stamina in performing hard labor and skill in using explosives, Chinese crews were recruited by hydraulic and quartz mining companies, which had replaced independent miners, to work as dynamiters and ditch diggers. They were also used to drain swamplands and build levees in the San Joaquin-Sacramento River deltas, and to construct roads, rock walls, and wine cellars in the Sonoma Valley. Chinese men made up the bulk of the labor force in the logging industry in the Sierra Nevada, salmon canneries in the Pacific Northwest, the hop fields and fruit orchards of California, and the cigar, shoe, and textile factories in San Francisco. In mining camps and towns throughout the West, Chinese men accepted jobs considered "women's work"—domestic servants, cooks, and laundrymen—that were shunned by white men, contributing to the stereotype of Chinese men as unmanly and effeminate.

Widely regarded as a reliable and cheap labor force, Chinese were recruited to construct regional railroad lines throughout the West. For a brief period, they were also sought after to work in the fields formerly tilled by black slaves in the South and to replace white workers on strike in factory towns in the East. In the 1880s, as anti-Chinese hostilities escalated in the West and the Chinese were driven out of the mines, factories, and fields, many Chinese moved eastward and to the Deep South, where they found an economic niche for themselves operating laundries, restaurants, and grocery stores. By 1900, one out of five employed Chinese men in America was a laundryman.

THE ROAD TO CHINESE EXCLUSION

Chinese—considered the dregs of humanity from a backward, heathen, despotic country—faced hostility in the United States almost from the start. Arriving at a time of Western expansion when Anglo Americans, imbued with a strong sense of Manifest Destiny and white supremacy, were laying sole claim to the lands and riches therein, Chinese immigrants fell victim to racial discrimination, economic exploitation, and political disenfranchisement. Although industrialists welcomed the labor they provided, nativists saw the newcomers as a racial, economic, and moral threat to white workers and American society. Racialized as innately inferior, akin to Africans, Native Americans, and Mexicans, Chinese were depicted in nineteenth-century popular culture as pig-tailed "coolies" who brought "filth, immorality, diseases, and ruin to white labor" (Documents 9–15). In a predominantly male society, prostitution was rampant in the West, but only Chinese prostitutes were blamed for spreading a deadly strain of venereal disease among white youths, and Chinese men were viewed as sexual predators who lured white women into their "dens of vice and depravity" (Document 10). Stereotyped as dishonest tricksters and idolatrous heathens with no commitment to American government and society (Document 8), Chinese were prohibited by California state law from testifying against white persons in court, marrying whites, and owning land, and by federal law from becoming U.S. citizens, and, ultimately, immigrating to the United States.

Racial discrimination and hostilities against the Chinese began in the mines during the Gold Rush. Under the nativist banner of "California for Americans," white miners had successfully driven out the French, Mexicans, and Chileans with the Foreign Miners' Tax or vigilante violence, but Chinese prospectors were still reaping profits from the low-yield claims that others had abandoned. In 1852, two years after California was admitted into the Union as a free state, Governor John Bigler, aiming to win the votes of white miners in the next election, became the first politician to call attention to the large influx of Chinese "coolies" and the need to ban them from working in the mines (Document 1). Norman Asing, a self-proclaimed "Chinaman, republican, and lover of free institutions," was quick to challenge Bigler's depictions of the Chinese as a degraded race in the *Daily Alta*, but to no avail (Document 2). That same year, the California legislature reenacted the Foreign Miners' Tax, with the intention of enforcing it directly against Chinese miners. Until it was voided by the Civil Rights Act of 1870, this tax accounted for $5 million or close to half of the state's revenue.[6] Many mining districts also passed special taxes and resolutions to exclude the Chinese, while hostile miners resorted to using physical violence to expel them from the diggings.

San Francisco, where many Chinese chose to settle, passed similar ordinances in the early 1870s intended to deprive Chinese of their livelihoods and make their lives so miserable that they would leave. The Sidewalk Ordinance prohibited Chinese peddlers from walking on sidewalks while using poles to carry their wares. Many Chinese were arrested and jailed for violating the Cubic Air Ordinance, which ordered 500 cubic feet of air per lodger in any dwelling. The Queue Ordinance required that the hair of prisoners be cut to within one inch of the scalp—a disgrace to Chinese whose queues represented their allegiance to the Chinese government.[7] There was even an ordinance against the Chinese custom of sending the bodies of their dead back to China. Chinese commonly fell victim to threats, assaults, robberies, and murder. In 1869, the abuse became so flagrant and the police so indifferent that the Chinese community hired their own police force to patrol the city day and night and to arrest anyone attacking the Chinese.

But the worst was yet to come as racial antagonism, combined with class tensions and party politics, coalesced into a national movement for Chinese exclusion. Rather than usher in an era of prosperity as anticipated, the completion of the transcontinental railroad in 1869 created economic problems for the Pacific Coast. Land values dropped, freight costs remained high, and unemployment rose as discharged railroad workers and cheaper manufactured products from the East poured into the West. The working classes blamed the railroads, corporations, and Chinese for their economic woes. From their perspective, Chinese workers were imported, unfair competition, lowering wages, and stealing their jobs. In retaliation, labor groups held anti-Chinese demonstrations and conventions, anti-coolie clubs organized boycotts against Chinese products, and mobs attacked Chinese settlements in the Western states. In 1871, one of the largest mass lynchings occurred in Los Angeles Chinatown, where a fight between two Chinese factions over a Chinese woman ended in two white officers being wounded and a civilian killed. A large mob rushed into the Chinese quarter, looting property, burning homes, and lynching those caught alive. Although eight men were convicted and sentenced to jail for the murder of nineteen Chinese residents, the U.S. Circuit Court overturned the conviction on a technicality and freed the murderers.

In December 1874, the anti-Chinese movement received a boost from President Ulysses S. Grant, who in his annual message to Congress charged that large proportions of Chinese immigrants were coming involuntarily to this country as contract laborers and prostitutes. With the intention to defuse labor unrest ensuing from the Panic of 1873 and at the same time secure the support of working-class voters for the Republican Party, Grant vowed to get rid of these "evils." A few days later, California congressman Horace Page (R) introduced a bill that would specifically prohibit the importation of Chinese contract laborers and prostitutes. Known as the Page Law of 1875, it passed both houses readily and marked the federal government's first step toward general Chinese exclusion. Although the new law did little to curtail the immigration of Chinese laborers, the stringent screening process it required of all "suspicious" women at the consular offices in Hong Kong did succeed in deterring female immigration from China and the establishment of Chinese family life in America.[8]

Political parties, vying to win the working-class vote in the Western states during the last quarter of the nineteenth century when every election was a close race, proved to be the most effective ally of the growing anti-Chinese forces. Until then, the Democratic Party had rehabilitated itself after the Civil War around the interests of the white working class in calling for high tariffs and Chinese exclusion while the Republican Party—the party of Abraham Lincoln that had freed the slaves—supported free trade, immigration, and racial equality. But in the closely contested election of 1876, the Republican Party chose self-interest over equal rights when it agreed to withdraw federal troops from the South in order to get their candidate Rutherford B. Hayes elected president. This compromise led to the collapse of Reconstruction and the unleashing of racial violence in the South. In the 1880 election, California and Nevada almost cost Republican candidate James A. Garfield the election when both Western states went Democratic in retaliation for President Hayes's veto of the first major piece of anti-Chinese immigration legislation. Once it became evident that anti-Chinese politics was successful politics, both parties adopted anti-Chinese platforms at election time. Politicians did the same when it came time to consider the question of Chinese exclusion in Congress. Chinese, possessing no vote, no political leverage whatsoever, held no sway over their decisions (Document 14).[9]

The year 1877 marked a crisis in the Chinese exclusion movement. The Long Depression prevailing for several years in the East hit the West hard, with local conditions made worse by a panic in silver stocks and two severe droughts in succession. Crops failed, real estate and corporate profits plummeted, wages fell, and the unemployment rate rose to 14 percent. Many unemployed miners and farmhands flocked to San Francisco for work, only to be met by the largest influx of Chinese immigrants since 1852. On July 23, racial hostilities broke out at a rally of some 6,000 workingmen who had assembled in the sandlot adjacent to the city jail to express support for the railroad strikes in the East. Anti-coolie sentiment was injected into the meeting, and an angry mob ransacked fifteen Chinese laundries nearby and viciously attacked any Chinese they encountered on the streets. This reign of terror lasted three days, resulting in four deaths, fourteen wounded, and twenty buildings looted and torched, before it was put to an end by a "Pick-Handle Brigade" of 4,000 volunteers.

That fall, workingmen from several labor organizations formed their own political party—the Workingmen's Party of California—specifically to take control of the government, destroy corporate monopolies, and rid the country of cheap Chinese labor. They elected Denis Kearney, an Irish Catholic immigrant in the drayage business, party president in the spring of 1878.[10] A gifted demagogue, Kearney gained attention on the sandlots of San Francisco with his harsh anti-Chinese rhetoric, often ending his speeches with the rallying cry of "The Chinese must go!" (Document 5). Recognizing the dire situation, the Chinese Six Companies, whose members represented prominent family and district associations, wrote memorials to Congress and President Hayes in late 1877 that aimed to present "the Chinese side of the question" and to remind them of U.S. obligations in the Burlingame Treaty of 1868 to protect their rights as citizens of the most favored nation.

In the next two years until its demise in 1879 due to factionalism, the Workingmen's Party made rapid progress in holding conventions and parades, organizing branches all over the state, and electing members to fill municipal offices. Its crowning achievement was reached in June 1878, when the Workingmen's Party won one-third of the seats in the state constitutional convention. During the drafting of California's second constitution (adopted in 1879), the party was able to push through measures that allowed the state to regulate immigration, prohibit the employment of Chinese by private corporations and public works, and authorize the removal of Chinese from cities and towns. Within a year of the constitution's ratification, all of these measures were ruled unconstitutional by the U.S. Circuit Court, and it became obvious to anti-Chinese activists in the West that federal action was needed to resolve the region's racial and class conflicts.

In an effort to convince the rest of the country to restrict Chinese immigration, the California state senate appointed a bipartisan committee to investigate the Chinese problem. Altogether sixty witnesses appeared before the committee, including twenty-two public officials and eighteen Chinese. Sorely missing were the testimonies of transportation companies, those with interest in China trade, and large landowners. The bipartisan committee's memorial to Congress, "An Address to the People of the United States upon the Evils of Chinese Immigration," confirmed largely negative opinions of the Chinese—that they were from the lowest orders with little respect for American laws, religion, and customs; that practically all of the women were prostitutes; that the bulk of Chinese labor had been imported under contract and posed a threat to free white labor; and that the Chinese were incapable of assimilating into American society. Recognizing the importance of U.S.–China trade to the country's economy, however, the committee was careful not to violate the provisions of the Burlingame Treaty. It recommended that Congress renegotiate the treaty and then pass legislation to limit Chinese immigration to ten persons on any one vessel. In response, Congress appointed and sent its own Joint Special Committee to the West Coast to investigate the problem of Chinese immigration. After listening to 130 people representing different sides of the question, the committee came to the same conclusions as the state senate committee.[11]

CONGRESS TAKES ACTION

The stage was set for Congress to act on California's cry for relief from the "evils of Chinese immigration." The Fifteen Passenger Bill of 1879, which limited vessels entering the country to carrying no more than fifteen Chinese passengers, passed in the Democratic-controlled House, 155 to 72, after only one hour of debate, and in the Senate, 139 to 27, after three days of debate. Senator James G. Blaine (R-ME), a distinguished public figure and prime contender for the Republican presidential nomination, was the first to break with pro-Chinese Republicans from the Northeast. Referring to the Naturalization Act of 1870, which rejected the possibility of Chinese citizenship, he argued that the country should not allow the immigration of anyone deemed unfit for citizenship. In conclusion, he said, "We can choose here today whether our legislation shall be in the interest of the American free laborer or for the servile laborer from China . . . whether we will have for the Pacific coast the civilization of Christ or the civilization of Confucius."[12] Senator Hannibal Hamlin (R-ME), who had served as Abraham Lincoln's first vice president and who was regarded as a party patriarch with enormous moral authority, led the fight against the bill on the grounds that it violated treaty provisions as well as the doctrine of equal rights. He believed in granting citizenship rights to all immigrants, including the Chinese. "I shall vote against this measure," he concluded, "and I leave that vote the last legacy to my children that they may esteem it the brightest act of my life."[13] President Hayes, when presented with the bill, vetoed it for violating the Burlingame Treaty and the harm it would inflict on commercial and missionary interests in China. An attempt to override the president's veto failed (Document 15).[14]

In an effort to remove the treaty roadblock, President Hayes sent a three-man commission under James B. Angell to China to modify the Burlingame Treaty. Anxious for American support in case of a military attack from Russia or Japan, Chinese officials agreed to almost everything the American delegation demanded. The Angell Treaty of 1880 permitted the United States to regulate, limit, or suspend, but not absolutely prohibit, the immigration of Chinese laborers. China was given assurances that teachers, students, merchants, and travelers for curiosity would be exempt from restriction and that all Chinese subjects in the United States would be protected from any mistreatment or abuse.

In the spring of 1882, Congress was ready to consider legislation to implement the new treaty agreement. Senator John F. Miller (R-CA) introduced Senate Bill 71, which was formally titled "An act to execute certain treaty stipulations relating to the Chinese," in the Senate.[15] The bill proposed to suspend the immigration of Chinese laborers, both skilled and unskilled, for twenty years, and prohibit the admission of Chinese to citizenship. Democrats and West Coast Republicans argued that Chinese exclusion was necessary to stop the influx of cheap labor and defend white America from the invasion of an inferior but vast race. With the failure of Reconstruction, the South no longer needed Chinese labor and Republicans were willing to support Chinese exclusion in exchange for support of black disenfranchisement and legal segregation in the South. Eastern and Midwestern Republicans, however, were divided on the issue. Some held fast to their republican ideals of equal rights and interests in China trade while others supported immigration restriction but objected to the harshness of the bill (Document 6). After fifteen days of contentious debate, the twenty-year exclusion bill passed the Senate, 20 to 15, and the House, 167 to 66.

While the bill was still being debated in Congress, mass meetings were held throughout the Pacific states, after which petitions and memorials in support of the bill poured in to Congress and the president, with labor groups predominating. Nevertheless, President Chester A. Arthur vetoed the bill on the grounds that the twenty-year period was contrary to the terms and spirit of the Angell Treaty and would damage U.S.–China trade. Immediately after the veto, a new bill was drawn up reducing the period to ten years. Wanting to end racial and class tensions and restore order in the nation, Republican opposition to Chinese exclusion in the Northeast gave way and the bill passed overwhelmingly in both houses with little debate, and President Arthur signed it into law on May 6, 1882 (Document 7).

The Chinese Exclusion Act, instead of defusing racial and class conflict on the Pacific Coast, worked in tandem with another economic downturn to unleash racial violence and brutality against the Chinese. As a result, the 1880s turned out to be the bloodiest decade for Chinese immigrants. There were ninety-one reported incidences of anti-Chinese purges involving murderous mobs that stormed Chinese settlements throughout the American West, looting, lynching, burning, and expelling Chinese. One of the worst outbreaks occurred in the mines at Rock Springs, Wyoming, in 1885. After Chinese miners there refused to join white miners in a strike for higher wages, a mob of armed white men opened fire on defenseless Chinese miners, killing twenty-eight and wounding fifteen, and burning all seventy-nine Chinese homes. None of the rioters were ever arrested and punished for their crimes, but after a thorough investigation of the massacre, Chinese minister Cheng Tsao Ju was able to persuade President Grover Cleveland and Congress to appropriate $150,000 to cover the property losses.[16]

Despite the anti-Chinese laws and racial violence, Chinese stood their ground and fought back via diplomatic and legal channels. The Chinese diplomatic corps, reminding the U.S. government of its treaty obligations to protect their rights, persons, and property, repeatedly protested the anti-Chinese laws and mistreatment of Chinese immigrants and demanded indemnities on their behalf. Community organizations like the Chinese Six Companies sent numerous memorandums to Congress and the president protesting their ill treatment. They also hired white attorneys to challenge dozens of anti-Chinese laws in federal court. Some notable successes like *Yick Wo v. Hopkins* (1886) and *Wong Kim Ark v. United States* (1898) became landmark cases in U.S. constitutional law.[17]

Chinese desperate to escape political and economic instability in China or eager to join families already in America did not take long to find ways to circumvent the exclusion laws. Some were smuggled into the country from Mexico or Canada. Others entered by falsely claiming exempt status or U.S. citizenship. When denied entry by immigrant inspectors, they appealed to the federal and state courts, which more often than not granted them admittance into the country. With 7,000 Chinese cases still pending in the federal courts during the 1886–1887 fiscal year, immigration officials admitted only ten Chinese immigrants into the United States, although 11,000 Chinese reportedly arrived in San Francisco with legal certificates.[18] Clearly, Chinese immigration had not been completely halted, and a public outcry ensued.

As complaints and demands poured in for more severe restrictions, Congress responded by passing additional laws to eliminate loopholes, track and control Chinese immigrants already in the country, and put a stop to immigration fraud. An amendment to the 1882 Exclusion Act in 1885 barred entry to Chinese laborers from other foreign countries and required that Section 6 certificates, issued by the Chinese government to the exempt classes, be endorsed by the U.S. consul. In 1888, Congress broadened the terms of exclusion. Instead of explicitly barring Chinese laborers, the new provisions excluded *all* Chinese except for "teachers, students, merchants, or travelers for pleasure or curiosity." The law also prohibited the return of any Chinese laborer unless he had family or assets and debts due him worth at least $1,000 in the United States. That same year, Congress passed the Scott Act, which abrogated all outstanding certificates of reentry issued to Chinese laborers, effectively barring the return of 20,000 Chinese to the United States.

The Geary Act of 1892 renewed Chinese exclusion for another ten years and required all Chinese to register for certificates of residence or risk imprisonment and deportation. Hedging their bets on a court decision that would rule the Geary Act unconstitutional on racial grounds, the Chinese Six Companies organized a campaign to discourage Chinese residents from registering. The Supreme Court, however, upheld the Geary Act. Rather than deport 100,000 Chinese at great expense, Congress passed the McCreary Amendment to extend the deadline for registration by six months. At the same time, the amendment restricted the definition of merchant to a person engaged in buying and selling merchandise—someone who did not perform any manual labor. Furthermore, a merchant had to produce two credible white witnesses in order to be readmitted into the country.

China had refused to ratify the Bayard-Zhang Treaty in 1888, which would have banned Chinese laborers from the United States for twenty years, including those who were returning from travels abroad. Their refusal had led Congress to hastily pass the Scott Act of 1888. The Chinese minister now proposed that if the United States would repeal the Scott Act, China would agree to the prohibition of Chinese laborers for ten years and to the registration of Chinese residing in the United States. Known as the Gresham-Yang Treaty, it basically sanctioned the Geary Act and was ratified by Congress in 1894.

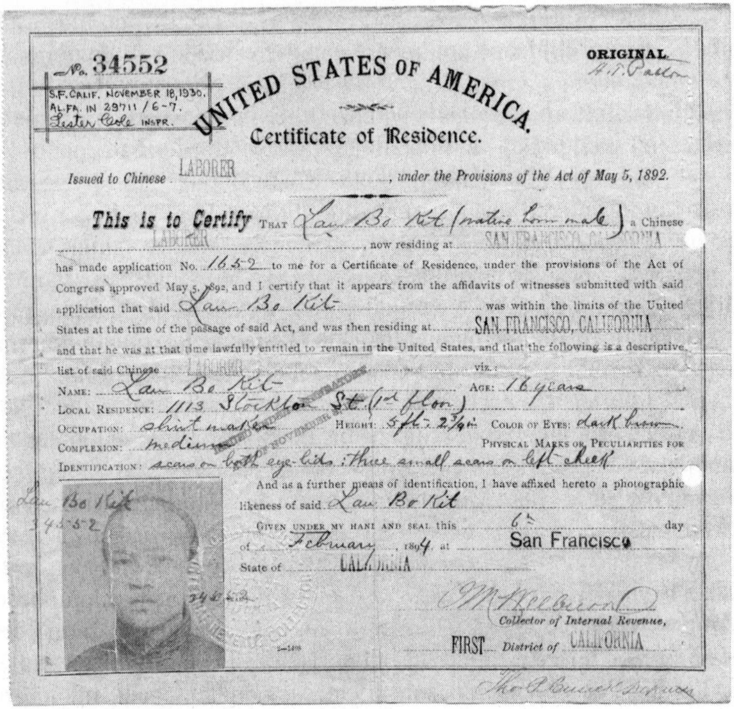

No. 34552

ORIGINAL.
H. T. Patton

S.F. CALIF. NOVEMBER 18, 1930.
AL. FA. IN 29711 / 6-7.
Lester Cole INSPR.

UNITED STATES OF AMERICA.
Certificate of Residence.

Issued to Chinese LABORER, under the Provisions of the Act of May 5, 1892.

This is to Certify THAT Lau Bo Kit (native born male) a Chinese LABORER, now residing at SAN FRANCISCO, CALIFORNIA has made application No. 1652 to me for a Certificate of Residence, under the provisions of the Act of Congress approved May 5, 1892, and I certify that it appears from the affidavits of witnesses submitted with said application that said Lau Bo Kit was within the limits of the United States at the time of the passage of said Act, and was then residing at SAN FRANCISCO, CALIFORNIA and that he was at that time lawfully entitled to remain in the United States, and that the following is a descriptive list of said Chinese LABORER viz.:

NAME: Lau Bo Kit AGE: 16 years
LOCAL RESIDENCE: 1113 Stockton St. (1st floor)
OCCUPATION: shirt maker HEIGHT: 5 ft. 2 3/4 in. COLOR OF EYES: dark brown
COMPLEXION: medium PHYSICAL MARKS OR PECULIARITIES FOR IDENTIFICATION: scars on both eye-lids: three small scars on left cheek

And as a further means of identification, I have affixed hereto a photographic likeness of said Lau Bo Kit

GIVEN UNDER MY HAND AND SEAL this 6th day of February, 1894, at San Francisco
State of CALIFORNIA

J. M. Welburn
Collector of Internal Revenue,
FIRST District of CALIFORNIA

Figure 1. *Certificate of Residence of Lau Bo Kit*
Chinese laborers were required by the Geary Act of 1892 to register with the federal government. Those found without a certificate of residence could be arrested and deported.
Courtesy of National Archives, San Francisco.

After the United States annexed the Hawaiian Islands and took control of the Philippines in 1898 as part of its efforts to dominate Pacific and Asian trade, Congress extended the Chinese exclusion laws to cover its new territories. Hence, Chinese immigration into the islands as well as their remigration to the United States was prohibited. In 1904, after China refused to renew the Gresham-Yang Treaty, Congress moved to make the exclusion laws permanent. By this last act, all Chinese laborers were prohibited from coming into the United States and its territories; those already here were permitted to leave and return only if they registered for a reentry certificate and had family or property valued at $1,000 in this country; Chinese officials, teachers, students, merchants, travelers for pleasure, U.S. citizens, and wives and children of these exempt classes were permitted to enter only under strict regulations; anyone who falsified identity papers or abetted an unlawful entry could be charged with a misdemeanor, fined, and imprisoned; and anyone found unlawfully in the United States could be arrested and deported.

ENFORCING THE EXCLUSION LAWS, 1882–1910

Once the United States passed the Chinese Exclusion Act, it faced the difficult task of enforcing it without a body of trained officers, bureaucratic machinery, or detention facility. The responsibility for inspecting Chinese immigrants at the ports of entry initially fell to the U.S. Customs Service under the direction of the secretary of treasury. A new post of "Chinese inspector" was created and charged with investigating all Chinese immigrants aboard arriving ships to determine their eligibility to enter the country. Usually, those holding Section 6 certificates from the Chinese government, which served as proof of their exempt status, or certificates issued by the collector at the port before departure were allowed to land immediately. However, if the inspector suspected any foul play, he could detain the applicant on the ship for further investigation.

Chinese passengers without documents—those claiming to be wives or offspring of U.S. citizens or merchants—were subjected to an interrogation in which they were asked detailed questions about their family history, village life, and relatives in America. Any notable discrepancies between their answers and those of their witnesses could be used as evidence of a false claim and cause for deportation. If denied entry, Chinese were allowed to appeal their cases to the secretary of treasury or to the federal district or state circuit courts. Between 1882 and 1905, Chinese filed over 9,600 writs of habeas corpus, alleging that they were entitled to land but were being unlawfully detained by the collector of customs. On average, the courts ruled in their favor over 50 percent of the time. But in 1905, this avenue was closed when the Supreme Court ruled in *Ju Toy v. United States* that the decision of the secretary of commerce and labor was final. Only for claims that immigration officers had abused their authority could Chinese now appeal the bureau's decisions in the courts.[19]

Until their cases were settled, Chinese immigrants were detained on the ship. If it took longer than a few days, they were transferred from one ship to another or kept in the county jail. Beginning in 1898, the

Pacific Mail Steamship Company converted its offices at Pier 40 into a detention shed to accommodate the large numbers of Chinese detainees. As many as five hundred immigrants at a time were crammed into the two-storied structure with no access to sunshine, fresh air, or exercise. After repeated complaints from Chinese community leaders that the facility was overcrowded, unsanitary, and a firetrap, immigration officials persuaded Congress to appropriate $250,000 in 1904 to build a new immigration station on Angel Island in San Francisco Bay.

During the first two decades of the exclusion era, the loose administrative structure of the Customs Service and the absence of a centralized immigration bureau gave customs officials in San Francisco free rein to develop and enforce regulations and procedures as they saw fit. As political appointees rather than civil service employees, they tended to cater to public opinion and party politics in strictly enforcing the exclusion laws. Many of the early immigration officials like John Wise, collector of customs from 1892 to 1898, and Terence V. Powderly, commissioner-general of immigration from 1897 to 1902, had strong ties to organized labor and the Chinese exclusion movement. Using the excuse of guarding against fraudulent entry, they made up new rules to hinder applicants and condoned raids in the Chinese community in order to arrest and deport illegal immigrants (Documents 16 and 17). In 1903, after Congress transferred the Bureau of Immigration to the newly created Department of Commerce and Labor, collectors of customs at the various ports of entry were replaced by officers of the bureau. Initially, the bureau continued to adopt anti-Chinese tactics, but over time, the immigration service was reformed. Nevertheless, with Chinese persisting in finding ways to enter the country unlawfully, a deep-rooted suspicion of Chinese immigrants permeated the bureau throughout the exclusion era, leading to more stringent measures to exclude them.[20]

The Chinese resisted exclusion every step of the way through evasion and legal appeals, diplomatic channels and public protest. A creative strategy that came to be known as "paper sons" was widely used by Chinese after the 1906 earthquake in San Francisco destroyed all birth records in City Hall. Chinese entering the country for the first time or returning from visits to China often claimed more sons than they actually had in order to create immigration slots that were sold to prospective immigrants called "paper sons"—individuals who were offspring not in reality but on paper only. On average, a paper son slot cost $100 per year of age or $1,500 to $2,000. Along with the false identity and papers came a coaching book that included answers to questions pertaining to family history, village life, and even personal habits. All newcomers committed the information to memory and knew to destroy the coaching book before they arrived in the United States, lest authorities find and use the books as evidence of fraudulent entry. Those who failed the interrogation and were denied entry spared no expense to hire attorneys to file appeals on their behalf. Chinese immigrants and immigration officials both estimated that 80 to 90 percent of Chinese applicants during the exclusion period (1882–1943) were most likely paper sons or paper daughters.

Among the most outspoken opponents of exclusion were Wu Ting-fang, Chinese minister to the United States from 1897 to 1901, and Ng Poon Chew, editor of the *Chung Sai Yat Po* (Chinese American daily newspaper). In defending the elite classes, both men took every opportunity to protest the Immigration Bureau's narrow definition and harsh treatment of the exempt classes, citing case after case of merchants and students who were unnecessarily detained, photographed, examined like criminals, and often denied entry on minor technicalities (Document 18). Not only were these actions a clear violation of treaty stipulations, but they were regarded by the Chinese as an affront to their race and national honor. Resentment turned to anger, culminating in the first national boycott of American goods in China. After the Gresham-Yang Treaty of 1894 expired and negotiations over its renewal stalled, Shanghai merchants boldly called for a boycott of American imports on March 16, 1905, in an effort to pressure the United States to modify its immigration policies toward the Chinese. Within a short time, the boycott, supported by merchants, students, and reformers in China as well as Chinese communities in Singapore, Japan, the Philippines, Hawaii, Cuba, Canada, and the United States, spread throughout China. It lasted ten months before the Chinese government caved in to political pressure from President Theodore Roosevelt and called a halt to the boycott.[21]

Although the boycott failed in getting the United States to modify the treaty, it did succeed in hurting U.S. trade and getting President Roosevelt, an advocate of eugenics and imperialism, to order immigration officers to treat *all* Chinese persons—laborers and the exempt classes—with courtesy or suffer immediate dismissal. He also moved to change the anti-Chinese personnel in the Department of Commerce and Labor by replacing Victor Metcalf, secretary of commerce and labor, with Oscar S. Straus, who had strong ties with pro-Chinese easterners and who went by the motto, "Make admission the rule and exclusion the exception" (Document 19). Straus made it a point to replace dishonest officers with new officers based on the results of civil service examinations. He also oversaw plans for erecting a new immigration station at Angel Island.

DETAINED ON ANGEL ISLAND, 1910–1940

On January 21, 1910, the "finest immigration station in the world" opened at Angel Island, a grass- and woodland-covered island in San Francisco Bay.[22] Modeled after the immigration station at Ellis Island, the location had been selected to prevent Chinese immigrants from being coached by friends and relatives on the outside as well as to protect Americans from contagious diseases that eugenicists believed Asians carried. Moreover, the immigration station, like Alcatraz prison nearby, was escape-proof. But soon after it opened, the government quickly discovered that the station's insular location was far from satisfactory. Fresh water was scarce, and the station was expensive to operate since all essentials had to be shipped from the mainland. Immigration officials criticized the buildings' shoddy construction and sanitary drawbacks, declaring them "virtual tinderboxes" and "unfit for habitation."[23] They proposed that the station be moved back to the mainland, but it was not until November 1940, after a fire destroyed the administration building, that the government finally abandoned the site and moved the immigration station to San Francisco.

Immigration Inspection

Known as the Ellis Island of the West, the Angel Island Immigration Station was a far cry from its counterpart in New York. Ellis Island was built in 1892 to welcome Europeans under laws that restricted their immigration but did not exclude them. Most arrivals at Ellis Island stayed only a few hours for a cursory physical exam and a brief interview intended to screen out undesirables. Ten percent of the twelve million immigrants to reach Ellis Island were detained for a few days for legal or medical reasons, and less than 2 percent were sent home in the end. In contrast, Angel Island was built to better enforce the Chinese exclusion laws—to keep out Chinese and, later, other Asian immigrants. At Angel Island, officials thoroughly examined and interrogated all Chinese newcomers, sending 5 percent home after being detained for several months at a time.

Two-thirds of the newcomers to Angel Island came from China and Japan, but there were also immigrants from other countries in Asia, Europe, Latin America, Africa, the Pacific Islands, and Australia.

From the moment that their ships landed in San Francisco, it became apparent that their treatment and their chances of being admitted into the country all hinged on immigration policies that discriminated against individuals on the basis of race, class, gender, and nationality. The differential treatment began during primary inspection, when immigration and medical officers climbed aboard the ships to inspect the papers and health of all the passengers and crew. First-class passengers, who were mostly white and wealthy, were given a cursory examination in the privacy of their cabins. They, along with returning residents and those traveling in second class, were usually allowed to land directly from the ship. Third-class and steerage passengers, who were mainly Asian and poor, along with sick passengers and anyone whose papers were in question, were all required to take the ferry to Angel Island for a more thorough inspection. Most non-Asians were thus able to avoid Angel Island altogether or had a very short stay. In contrast, all Chinese newcomers were transported to Angel Island and detained there for long periods of time while awaiting decisions on their applications.[24]

Upon arriving at Angel Island, passengers had to deposit their luggage in the baggage shed and were then shepherded to the immigration station, where segregation policies were strictly enforced to avoid confusion and collusion, as well as to protect whites from the "contamination" of Asians. Men and women, including husbands and wives, were separated and not allowed to see or communicate with each other until their cases had been settled. Children under age twelve were assigned to the care of their mothers. There were also separate living quarters, dining halls and eating times, recreation areas, and hospital entrances and wards—all designed to keep the different classes, races, and genders apart. Superior detention quarters and dining facilities and better food and treatment for whites reflected the racial favoritism embedded in the U.S. immigration policies.

The first stop for the new arrivals was the administration building, which housed the registration rooms, offices, medical exam room, four dining halls, dormitories for employees, and detention quarters for one hundred people. There they were segregated into waiting areas, given a quick look-over, registered, and assigned to their living quarters. Chinese and Japanese men were kept in separate sections of the detention building; all others, including women and children, were housed on the second floor of the administration building in segregated quarters.

The next day, they were taken to the hospital, located northeast of the administration building, for the medical exam. While non-Asians were given a cursory line inspection and eye exam for any medical defects or signs of trachoma, Asian immigrants were subjected to a more intensive and invasive exam of their blood and waste products for traces of intestinal parasites that they were racially presumed to carry. According to the Act of March 3, 1891, immigrants could be excluded for having such "loathsome and dangerously contagious diseases" as trachoma, tuberculosis, syphilis, gonorrhea, and leprosy. In 1910, unc-inariasis (hookworm infection) and filariasis (threadworm infection) were added to the list of excludable diseases, and in 1917, clonorchi-asis (liver fluke infection) was also classified as reason for exclusion. Because of poor sanitation in rural parts of Asia, immigrants from China, Japan, Korea, and India were most commonly diagnosed with these parasitic diseases and denied entry. The men were required to strip naked in order to reveal any abnormalities. Women were not required to disrobe unless the doctors detected specific signs of disease. However, if there were any doubts about the claimed age of any

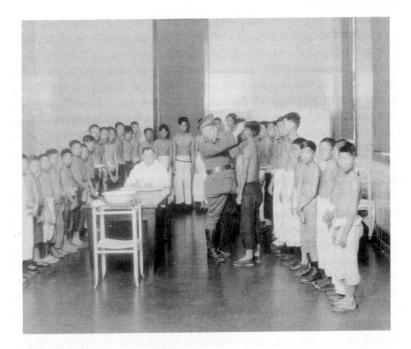

Figure 2. *Medical examination in the hospital building at Angel Island*
Courtesy of National Archives, Washington, D.C.

Chinese applicant, both male and female applicants were subjected to a nude inspection of their body parts, which caused many Chinese, unaccustomed to exposing themselves in public, to feel humiliated and angry (Documents 23 and 24).[25]

The Chinese reacted strongly to these discriminatory procedures. An editorial in the *Chinese Defender* sarcastically accused the Public Health Service of inventing the hookworm diagnosis as a way of barring Chinese entry to the country. "So arriving immigrants now have hookworms. Somebody must have stayed awake nights to think that out; it surely was a stroke of genius!"[26] After considerable protest from Chinese organizations and among diplomatic circles, the U.S. government reclassified the parasitic diseases and allowed immigrants to seek medical treatment at the immigration hospital, but at their own expense. Asian immigrants thus had higher rates of medical exclusion, longer stays on the island, and more added expenses than their European counterparts. Those fortunate to pass the medical hurdle returned to their dormitories to await the dreaded interrogation on their application.

Board of Special Inquiry Hearing

During the early years of the immigration station's operations, this waiting period could stretch into months, which became a source of many complaints. During the mid-1920s, detention averaged two to three weeks. The Chinese also complained that the examination procedure for Chinese applicants and witnesses was unfair. In response, the Immigration Service modified regulations to require that Chinese cases be heard by Boards of Special Inquiry instead of a single inspector. This change seemed to put Chinese on the same footing with other aliens. But the board, consisting of two immigrant inspectors and a stenographer, was allowed to use any means it deemed fit to ascertain the legitimacy of a Chinese applicant's right to enter the United States under the Chinese exclusion acts as well as general immigration laws. For Chinese applicants, this meant longer and more exhaustive interrogations than for any other immigrant group on Angel Island.

Chinese immigrants entering the country as merchants had to provide detailed documentation of their business activities and volume of merchandise, a list of all partners, and produce two white witnesses to testify on their behalf. The applicant's appearance, handwriting, clothing, and hands (whether calloused or smooth) were all used as evidence to determine whether they were bona fide merchants or laborers in disguise. Even after admission, a merchant's dealings with

Figure 3. *A Chinese applicant being interrogated at Angel Island, 1916*
Courtesy of National Archives, Washington, D.C.

the Immigration Service did not end. All Chinese businesses were required to send an up-to-date list of their partners to immigration authorities on a regular basis, and investigators were often sent into the Chinese community to ascertain whether merchants were maintaining the exempt status under which they had been admitted. If they were not, they could face arrest and deportation.

By the 1920s, more Chinese were using the "paper son" strategy to claim derivative citizenship than any other immigration status. Because there were usually no documents to corroborate or disprove these claims, the Board of Special Inquiry confined evidence to the detailed testimony given by an applicant and his witnesses concerning family history, relationships, living arrangements, and everyday life in the village. Applicants were sometimes asked to identify family pictures and draw maps of their ancestral villages and the surrounding countryside. Any discrepancies in the answers of the applicant and the witness could mean exclusion and deportation. In the absence of any witnesses, as in the case of a returning native U.S. citizen who claimed to have left for China at a young age, authorities tested English-language proficiency and recollections of street names, public buildings, and important historical events.

Chinese women, who were entering the country primarily as the dependent wives or daughters of a merchant or U.S. citizen, were given a harder time than the men. They had to first prove to immigration officers that their husbands or fathers still qualified as members of the exempt classes. They had to also prove that their identities and relationships were real (Documents 24 and 25). Lacking official records of their births or marriages, the women were required to answer detailed and intimate questions about their living environments and marital relations. Women suspected of being prostitutes or having committed an act of "moral turpitude" were subjected to longer interviews and asked more intrusive questions about their sexual history than were men.

From the beginning, it was a game of cat and mouse in which some inspectors were strict but fair, others delighted in matching wits with the applicant, and still others used intimidation to test applicants. To immigration officials, such actions were necessary to ferret out discrepancies and fraud (Document 21). Chinese, however, viewed the dreaded interrogation process as unreasonable and harsh (Documents 23 and 24). Some queries would have been difficult for anyone to answer: What are the birth and marriage dates of your parents? How many times a year did you receive letters from your father? How many steps are there leading to your attic? Who lived in the third house in the second row of houses in your village? How many guests were at your wedding? Real sons and daughters, even those who had studied coaching books beforehand, sometimes failed the test.

Because Chinese immigrants usually did not understand English and the inspectors did not speak Chinese, the board provided an interpreter at the hearing. Beginning in 1898, the hiring of Chinese as interpreters was expressly prohibited because government officials believed that they could not be trusted in immigration work. By the time the Angel Island Immigration Station opened in 1910, government policies had changed, partly because it was almost impossible to find qualified whites to fill the positions. Most of the Chinese interpreters like Edwar Lee had college degrees, spoke a number of Chinese dialects, and came highly recommended by trustworthy white Americans like Donaldina Cameron, superintendent of the Presbyterian Mission Home in San Francisco. Even so, to forestall collusion between the applicant, witness, and interpreter, the board used a different interpreter for each session of the hearing. At the end of each session, the board chairman usually asked the interpreter to identify the dialect being spoken in order to ascertain whether the applicant and witnesses alleged to be members of the same family were speaking the same dialect. Chinese interpreters had no say in the board's final decision, but their attitudes and demeanor at the hearings could help or hinder applicants during the interrogation (Document 22).

Corruption in the Immigration Service was pervasive throughout the country, and it was no different at Angel Island. Immigrant inspectors and interpreters were known to accept bribes to render favorable decisions and interpretations. One of the biggest scandals broke in 1917 when a federal grand jury exposed a smuggling ring that was netting hundreds of thousands of dollars each year. Employees at Angel Island were caught stealing and manipulating Chinese records in connection with illegal entries. Duplicate copies of records were being sold to Chinese for $100 and immigrant inspectors were charging $200 for substituting a photograph in a Chinese file. The grand jury indicted thirty people, including immigrant inspectors, lawyers, and Chinese immigration brokers. As a result of the investigation, twenty-five employees were dismissed, transferred, or forced to resign.[27]

A typical proceeding usually lasted two or three days, longer if witnesses had to be interviewed in distant cities or if applicants and witnesses had to be recalled and reinterrogated about inconsistencies in their answers. Applicants were asked two hundred to one thousand questions, and transcripts ran between twenty and eighty typewritten pages. During these hearings, memories might fail, wrong answers might be given, and unforeseen questions might be asked. Hence, it was often necessary to smuggle coaching information into the detention quarters to resolve any discrepancies. One method was to hide coaching notes in gift packages sent by relatives in the city. Immigration officials who routinely inspected letters and packages found contraband messages inside hollow oranges, bananas, pork buns, and even peanuts, the shells having been pried apart and glued back together again. A second method involved the Chinese kitchen staff stopping by specified stores in Chinatown on their days off to pick up coaching messages left by relatives of detainees. For a small fee, they would smuggle the messages into the station and pass them at mealtimes to officers of the Angel Island Liberty Association, a mutual aid organization that Chinese male detainees formed in 1916.[28] The note was then taken upstairs to the detention barracks and delivered to the designated person (Document 20).

In the event that someone was caught passing a note, everyone was instructed to help destroy the evidence. One such incident made the headlines of the *San Francisco Chronicle* on March 30, 1928. While escorting a young Chinese woman to the dining room as the men were leaving, Chief Matron Mary L. Green saw the woman pick up a folded piece of paper dropped by one of the men. As soon as she seized the message from the girl and hid it in her dress, the men quickly turned and pounced on her. According to the newspaper account of the incident, "Fifty Chinese men attacked Mary L. Green. They tore at her dress, ripping it away from her chest and body, fingers scratching the flesh, hands pummeling the woman's arms and shoulder—seeking at any cost a mysterious note. The men found the note, tore it to bits. Then the bits disappeared, chewed and swallowed by the Orientals." Another riot was reported in the *San Francisco Chronicle* on July 2, 1925, when Chinese detainees beat up a white attendant for being an informer. Soldiers from Fort McDowell were called in to subdue the rioters with fixed bayonets.

If the applicant's testimony was largely corroborated by his witnesses, the authorities would render a favorable decision and land him or her. An unfavorable decision resulted in deportation unless the applicant chose to appeal the decision to higher authorities in Washington, DC, or the federal courts. Of all the immigrant groups on Angel Island, the Chinese were the most adept at taking advantage of the legal channels open to them. Many hired well-known immigration attorneys such as Joseph P. Fallon, George A. McGowan, Alfred L. Worley, and Oliver P. Stidger to prepare their applications and represent them at Angel Island and in the appeals. From 1910 to 1924, immigrant inspectors on Angel Island rejected 9 percent of the Chinese applicants. Of these, 88 percent retained attorneys to appeal the decisions, and 55 percent of the appeals were successful. In many cases, higher authorities ruled that the interrogation process at Angel Island had been unfair. Only 5 percent of all Chinese applicants ended up being deported, but because of the lengthy appeal process, 6 percent of the immigrants languished on Angel Island for more than a year before their cases were finally decided.[29]

Only one other immigrant group, South Asians, had a higher deportation rate than the Chinese. Primarily Sikhs and single men from the

Punjab districts of India, they had left their homes to escape British colonialism and poverty. Arriving at a time of intense anti-Asian sentiment, they had the highest rejection rate even though there was no exclusion law against them until Congress passed the Asian Barred Zone in 1917. From 1911 to 1915, 55 percent of all South Asian applicants were rejected, usually on grounds that they had hookworms or were "likely to become a public charge," a clause in the general immigration laws that applied to applicants with little funds or chances of finding employment. Unlike the Chinese, few South Asians had the financial resources to appeal their cases in court. They also did not have the support and assistance of a large ethnic community in America or the protection of a strong home government. Hence, the overwhelming majority were deported back to India.[30]

At the opposite extreme, Japanese applicants had the shortest stay and the lowest rate of deportation of all immigrant groups (under 1 percent), because Japan, having defeated China and Russia in two separate wars, was then a powerful nation. In 1907, to forestall Congress from passing legislation against Japanese immigration, the Japanese government negotiated an understanding with the United States known as the Gentlemen's Agreement, whereby Japan would stop issuing passports to laborers. This agreement permitted all Japanese aliens in the United States to send for their wives and children, a privilege denied Chinese laborers under the Chinese Exclusion Act. Armed with Japanese passports, birth and marriage records proving their right to enter the country, the overwhelming majority — including ten thousand picture brides — were admitted into the United States within a day or two of their arrival. But in 1924, Japanese immigration was halted by the National Origins Quota Act. Based on eugenicist beliefs in Nordic superiority, this new law restricted immigration from Eastern and Southern European countries and barred all "aliens ineligible for citizenship," namely Asians.[31]

According to the testimony of former detainees, quite a few Chinese were known to have committed suicide in the detention barracks or aboard returning ships, but research has revealed only a handful of cases. On October 7, 1918, the *San Francisco Chronicle* reported that Fong Fook, who was en route from China to Mexico, hanged himself with a towel tied to a gas fixture after a few days in detention. Lester Tom and Gerald Won, two boys who were detained on Angel Island in 1931 and 1936, respectively, recalled witnessing the suicides of two men who hanged themselves in the lavatory because they could not face the prospect of deportation. Interpreter Edwar Lee told oral historians the story of a Chinese woman who was so distraught about being deported that "she sharpened a chopstick and stuck it in her brain through the ear" and died (Document 22). Poems carved into the barrack walls also attest to the deaths and suicides of fellow detainees, but the exact number of suicides remain unknown.

Daily Life in Detention

At any one time, between two hundred and three hundred Chinese males and thirty to fifty Chinese females were detained at Angel Island. Most were new arrivals, but some were returning residents with questionable documents. Also confined were earlier arrivals whose applications had been denied and who were awaiting decisions on their appeals, Chinese residents who had been arrested and sentenced to be deported, and transients en route to and from countries neighboring the United States, especially Mexico and Cuba. In 1932, for example, the detention center held more than four hundred Chinese refugees from Mexico waiting to be deported to China because of Mexico's Expulsion Order.[32]

The men were kept in two large rooms of the detention building under lock and key, with wire-meshed windows and barbed-wire fences to prevent escape. The rooms were dark, poorly ventilated, and filled with rows of triple-deck metal bunks to accommodate 192 persons in each room. Privacy was minimal. According to one study by the Public Health Service, the crowded conditions were unsanitary and conducive to the spread of communicable diseases like meningitis.[33] Chinese women, originally detained in the same building, were moved to the second story of the administration building sometime before 1911. The daily routine for both men and women was marked by "wake-up" calls in the morning, three meals a day in the dining hall of the administration building, and "lights out" in the evening.

Guards stationed outside the dormitories generally left the Chinese alone. Confined inside, men languished on their bunks, spending their waking hours daydreaming or worrying about their futures. Some passed the time gambling, but stakes were usually small because inmates had little money. The literate read Chinese newspapers sent from San Francisco and books brought from home. By the late 1920s, a phonograph, Chinese opera records, and musical instruments purchased by the Angel Island Liberty Association were also available to break the monotony. A separate, fenced, outdoor recreation yard that was open for most of the day except during the rainy season afforded the men limited fresh air and exercise. Once a week, detainees were escorted to the baggage shed at the dock, where they could select needed items from their luggage (Document 23).

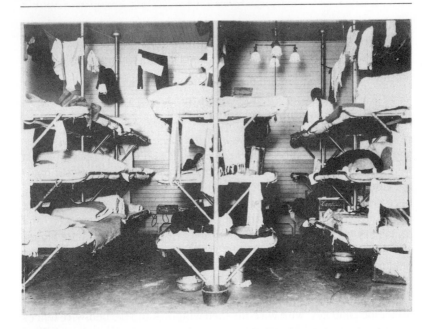

Figure 4. *Chinese men's dormitory, 1910*
Courtesy of California State Parks. Image 090–469.

Women marked their time in detention differently. Many lacked formal education and were unable to read Chinese newspapers and books sent from San Francisco. Some knitted or did needlework. A few attended English-language and Americanization classes organized by social workers. Women and children were periodically allowed to walk the grounds in a supervised group, a privilege denied Chinese men. Women, unlike the men, did not form an organization, but they supported one another by sharing food that had been sent by relatives in San Francisco, reading and writing letters for those who were illiterate, consoling the aggrieved, and accompanying one another to the lavatory for fear of seeing the ghosts of women who had committed suicide there (Document 24).

Unlike the other nationalities, Chinese were not allowed visitors until their cases had been settled, lest they collude on the interrogations. Other than immigration officials, the outsider they saw most often was Deaconess Katharine Maurer, who had been appointed in 1912 by the Women's Home Missionary Society of the Methodist

Figure 5. *Deaconess Katharine Maurer waiting with Chinese women in the registration area of the administration building*
Courtesy of California Historical Society.

Episcopal Church to tend to the welfare and needs of all immigrants on Angel Island. Her work was also supported by funds and gifts from the Daughters of the American Revolution. Maurer, who became known as the "Angel of Angel Island" and who was called "Ma" by the Chinese women, helped detainees write letters, taught them English, organized Christmas parties, and provided women and children with toiletries, clothing, sewing and knitting materials, books, and toys. Until she retired in 1951, she also distributed Bibles and promoted Christianity at the immigration station.

The San Francisco Chinese YMCA also made regular visits to the men's detention barracks to show movies, teach English, provide newspapers and recreational equipment, and prepare the immigrants for life in America. Chinese clergymen often came on these visits to preach to the inmates. Sometimes, staff from the Chinese YWCA would visit the women. However, neither Maurer nor these visitors could change the prisonlike conditions created by discriminatory exclusion laws, and, despite their persistence, they converted few inmates to Christianity.

The Chinese held at Angel Island understandably resented their long confinement, particularly because they knew that immigrants from other countries, like Japan and Russia, were processed and released within a day or two. Their disgruntlement was fueled by the enforced idleness and dismal conditions at the station. One major complaint was the food that they were served. At first, they complained about it being Western instead of Chinese food. After the Immigration Service started hiring Chinese cooks to prepare Chinese meals for them, they complained that the food was inedible. One reason was that the government awarded concessions for providing meals to private firms based on competitive bids, with the stipulation that less money be spent on meals for Asian detainees than for Europeans or employees. In 1916, the average cost per Chinese meal dropped from 14 cents to 8 cents, and the quality of food got worse. In response, male detainees protested by staging a disturbance in the dining hall, turning over their bowls and throwing utensils and food at the guards. There were enough of these disturbances to precipitate the posting of a sign in Chinese warning diners not to make trouble or spill food on the floor. In 1919, a full-fledged riot broke out and federal troops had to be called in from Fort McDowell to restore order. A year later, authorities in Washington, DC, finally decided to improve the situation, and the station began to serve better food.

Many discouraged applicants vented their frustrations and lodged their protests by writing Chinese poems on the walls as they waited for the results of their appeals. To date, over two hundred Chinese poems have been found on the walls of the detention building, along with thirty-three graphic images and three hundred inscriptions or signatures in eight foreign languages. Because Chinese women were kept in the administration building that was destroyed in the 1940 fire, there is no record of poems written by women, but Lee Puey You recalled seeing "sad and bitter poems" on the walls of the women's lavatory and she herself wrote poems while detained for twenty months at Angel Island (Document 24). All the poems were written by Cantonese villagers in their late teens with only a grammar school education. Yet they knew how to express themselves in the classical style of Chinese poetry, written with four or eight lines per poem and five or seven characters per line. In this form, the Chinese character at the end of every even-numbered line usually rhymes. The better poems, filled with historical and literary allusions and personal expressions of longing, anguish, and despair, show remarkable talent, maturity, and wisdom beyond the years of their creators. Almost all of the poems are undated and unsigned, most likely for fear of retribution from the authorities.

As the earliest literary expressions of Chinese immigrants, these poems not only bear witness to the indignities the immigrants suffered in coming to Gold Mountain but also serve as a reminder of the futility and folly of the exclusion laws themselves (Documents 23 and 27).[34]

ADDRESSING "A HISTORIC MISTAKE"

The irony of Chinese exclusion was that it did not improve the white workingman's lot. In reality, Chinese laborers were never a threat. At the peak of their immigration, they numbered less than 1 percent of the nation's population. Unemployment remained high and the wage level did not rise after the "cheap" competition had virtually been eliminated. In 1943, Congress addressed what President Franklin D. Roosevelt called "a historic mistake" by passing the Magnuson Act, which repealed the Chinese exclusion laws as a goodwill gesture to China, a U.S. ally in World War II (Document 28). Based on the National Origins Quota Act of 1924, however, only 105 persons of the Chinese race were permitted to immigrate annually to the United States, compared to the annual quota of 34,007 for Britain, another war ally. But Chinese immigrants were finally allowed to become U.S. citizens.

Given the small annual quota of 105, Chinese continued to use the paper son strategy to immigrate to the United States as derivative citizens, and the Immigration and Nationality Services (INS) continued to look for ways to stop them. In 1950, after the United States broke off diplomatic relations with "Communist China," immigration inspection of Chinese applicants was shifted from the port of entry to the American consulate in Hong Kong, and a year later, blood tests were introduced to detect false paternity claims. With the passage of the McCarran-Walter Act of 1952 during the Cold War, new procedures were established to screen out and deport "Communist infiltrators" and put an end to the paper son scheme. The INS established the Confession Program (1956–1965), whereby Chinese who admitted to their fraudulent entry could have their status adjusted and their real names restored. Working with the FBI, the INS attempted to force confessions by conducting immigration raids in Chinatowns and subpoenaing family and district association records for any proof of fraudulent entry. The program wreaked havoc in the Chinese community as the FBI went after Communist sympathizers. Those who confessed were asked to name their real and fictive families and often, other unlawful immigrants. Few Chinese were actually deported, but the INS considered the Confession Program one of its greatest achievements: 11,336

Chinese Americans confessed to fraudulent entry, implicating another 19,124 persons and closing 5,800 unused "paper son" slots.[35]

It was not until Congress passed the Immigration and Nationality Act of 1965 that racist quotas created by the National Origins Quota Act of 1924 were replaced with a system based on equal quotas for all countries and a preference for family reunification. The immigration gates opened, ushering in a surge of immigrants from Latin America and Asia. As a result, the Chinese population in the United States doubled every decade, growing from 237,000 in 1960 to 3.3 million in 2010. Families were reunited, and a new generation of Chinese Americans emerged.

The irreparable damage of Chinese exclusion and detention has been deep and long-lasting. It separated families for decades, reduced immigration and economic opportunities, and diminished civil rights. During the exclusion period, the Chinese population in America declined by 25 percent while the European population doubled. Paper sons and paper daughters had to live out their lives under false identities, in constant fear of detection by immigration authorities. Unpleasant memories as well as their shaky legal status led many Chinese to fear the law, to avoid any political activities, and to hide the truth about their immigration past from their children. Moreover, the feeling that they were allowed into this country only at the sufferance of the dominant white majority worked to foster alienation and delay their assimilation into mainstream society. Most damaging have been the psychological wounds inflicted by exclusion upon generations of Chinese Americans—the implication that they are racial inferiors, perpetual foreigners, and second-class citizens at best.

The Chinese Exclusion Act also had lasting consequences for U.S. immigration policy and the ways in which Americans think about race and immigration. It transformed America from being a nation with an open-door immigration policy to a gatekeeping nation that sought to protect itself from undesirable and dangerous aliens. Enforcing the Chinese exclusion laws set in motion new modes and technologies of immigration regulation, including immigrant inspectors and detention facilities, immigration documents like U.S. passports and "green cards," border patrols, immigration raids, and deportation policies—all standard practices in use today. After 1882, the list of who was considered "undesirable" and a racial threat to the nation grew as Congress increasingly used the law to exclude other Asian groups, restrict immigration from Southern and Eastern European countries, and deport Mexicans and Filipinos during the Great Depression. In the process, the very definition of "American" remained exclusively white.

On the 130th anniversary of the Chinese Exclusion Act of 1882, and at the urging of key Chinese American organizations, the Senate and the House of Representatives unanimously passed resolutions "expressing regret" for the Chinese Exclusion Act and reaffirmed their commitment to protecting the civil rights of all people (Document 29). Senate Resolution 201 and House Resolution 683 came too late for those who were most directly affected by the exclusion laws. But by acknowledging a legislative mistake, Congress made it possible for Chinese Americans to come out from the dark shadows of their immigration past, and for the nation as a whole to come to terms with the harm and injustice of the Chinese exclusion laws.

Yet the question "Have we learned from the injustices and mistakes of our past?" reverberates in the twenty-first century. Appealing to fears about economic uncertainty and national security, the Trump administration implemented restrictive immigration reform within the first year of taking office. These policies excluded immigrants from certain Muslim countries, cracked down on undocumented immigrants and Mexican "criminals" coming across the border, and sought to end "chain migration" of relatives in an effort to keep America white. Chinese Americans, who know too well the tragic consequences of the exclusion laws, were swift to take action. On May 6, 2017, the 135th anniversary of the Chinese Exclusion Act, a thousand people gathered at a Rally for Inclusion in the heart of San Francisco Chinatown to show solidarity with Muslims, immigrants, and refugees who were being targeted and to call upon Congress to make good on their promise to uphold the Constitution and protect the civil rights of all people. Their message rang loud and clear: "Remember 1882! Excluding immigrants on the basis of race and nationality was wrong then and it's wrong now!"[36] As we search for a way to fix our broken immigration system, we would do well to heed the lessons of Chinese exclusion and remember to uphold our values as a nation of immigrants with liberty and justice for all.

NOTES

[1]On the international context of Asian emigration, see Cheng and Bonacich, *Labor Immigration under Capitalism*; Chan, *Asian Americans*; and Lee, *The Making of Asian America*.

[2]The Treaty of Wangxia, signed between the United States and China in 1844, already granted the United States the same commercial benefits as Britain. The Burlingame Treaty, negotiated by Anson Burlingame, former American minister to China, accorded China the status of "most favored nation" and permitted the free movement of Chinese to the United States.

[3]The term "coolie" in Chinese means "unskilled laborer for hire." Used in conjunction with the "coolie trade," it refers to Chinese laborers who were coerced into signing contracts to work for a term of service at a fixed rate of wages under brutal slave-like conditions. This second meaning of the term was widely used pejoratively by anti-Chinese agitators to mischaracterize Chinese labor as unfree and unfair competition and thereby to justify their exclusion. For more on the coolie question, see Coolidge, *Chinese Immigration*, Chapter 3.

[4]On the immigration of Chinese women and prostitution, see Yung, *Unbound Feet*; and Hirata, "Free, Indentured, Enslaved."

[5]Sabin, *Building the Pacific Railway*, 111.

[6]Coolidge, *Chinese Immigration*, 36.

[7]Beginning in the Qing dynasty (1644–1911), Chinese men were required to dress their hair in a queue, or braided pigtail, as a sign of submission to the Manchu rulers or suffer the penalty of death.

[8]On the Page Act, see Peffer, *If They Don't Bring Their Women Here*.

[9]On the political causes of Chinese exclusion, see Gyory, *Closing the Gate*; and Zhu, *The Road to Chinese Exclusion*.

[10]More than any other ethnic group, Irish workers felt directly threatened by the Chinese in California in the 1870s for displacing them in manufacturing, laundering, and domestic occupations. Thus, Irish labor politicians like Denis Kearney, who also wanted to claim whiteness as their racial identity, were at the forefront of the anti-Chinese movement. See Lee, *Orientalism*, 67–72.

[11]See California State Senate, *Chinese Immigration*; and U.S. Senate, *Report of the Joint Senate Committee to Investigate Chinese Immigration*.

[12]8 *Congressional Record* 1303 (1879).

[13]8 *Congressional Record* 1387 (1879).

[14]On the legislative history of the Chinese Exclusion Act, see Gold, *Forbidden Citizens*.

[15]The term "Chinese Exclusion Act" would not appear in a bill title until 1943, when the Magnuson Act repealed all such anti-Chinese legislation.

[16]On Chinese expulsions, see Pfaelzer, *Driven Out*.

[17]In *Yick Wo v. Hopkins*, regarding a city ordinance that discriminated against Chinese laundries, the Supreme Court ruled that the equal protection clause of the Fourteenth Amendment covered all persons, including Chinese aliens. In *Wong Kim Ark v. United States*, concerning an American-born Chinese who was refused reentry into the country, the court held that regardless of race or the immigration status of one's parents, all persons born in the United States were citizens and could not be stripped of their rights.

[18]Coolidge, *Chinese Immigration*, 212, 500.

[19]On the legal history of Chinese exclusion, see Salyer, *Laws Harsh as Tigers*.

[20]On the strict enforcement of the Chinese exclusion laws, see Lee, *At America's Gates*.

[21]On the 1905 boycott, see McKee, *Chinese Exclusion versus the Open Door Policy*; and Tsai, *China and the Overseas Chinese in the United States*.

[22]*San Francisco Chronicle*, August 18, 1907, 4.

[23]*San Francisco Chronicle*, August 8, 1920, 52, and November 1, 1922, 8.

[24]For a comprehensive and comparative history of immigrant groups at Angel Island, see Lee and Yung, *Angel Island*.

[25]On the medical exams at Angel Island, see Shah, *Contagious Divides*.

[26]*Chinese Defender*, November 1910, 1.

[27]Lee, *At America's Gates*, 200.

[28]Also known as the Self-governing Association (Zizhihui), the Angel Island Liberty Association maintained order in the barracks, provided entertainment and recreational equipment, and negotiated with the authorities over any complaints or requests from detainees.

[29]See statistical tables compiled from INS sources in Lai, Lim, and Yung, *Island*, 2nd ed., 341–42.

[30]On the experiences of immigrants from India at Angel Island, see Lee and Yung, *Angel Island*, Chapter 4.

[31]On the experiences of Japanese immigrants at Angel Island, see Lee and Yung, *Angel Island*, Chapter 3. The Quota Acts of 1921 and 1924 placed numerical limitations on immigration for the first time and set quotas for each immigrant group based on national origin. Eugenicists at the time believed that one's place of birth and racial origin determined the quality of one's intellect, moral character, and assimilability into American society. They placed Nordics at the apex and argued that selectivity in human breeding and immigration would weed out the less desirable races. Thus, both quota laws were designed to encourage immigrants from Western Europe, block all but a few from Southern and Eastern Europe, and bar altogether those from Asia.

[32]Camacho, *Chinese Mexicans*, 86. See Document 27, *A Chinese Poem Left by a Deportee*, this volume, 00.

[33]See Bolton, "Cerebrospinal Meningitis at Angel Island Immigration Station."

[34]See Architectural Resources Group, "Poetry and Inscriptions," and Lai, Lim, and Yung, *Island*, for English translations of the poems, and go to www.aiisf.org to listen to poems read in Taishanese, Cantonese, and Mandarin Chinese.

[35]On the Confession Program, see Zhao, *Remaking Chinese America*, Chapter 7; and Ngai, "Legacies of Exclusion."

[36]See Yung, "Trump's Anti-Immigrant Campaign: Will We Repeat a Historic Mistake?" http://nomoreexclusion.org/unity-statement/.

PART TWO

The Documents

1

The Road to Exclusion

1

JOHN BIGLER

Governor's Special Message

April 23, 1852

*Printer, lawyer, and politician, John Bigler was born in Carlisle,
Pennsylvania, to parents of German ancestry in 1805. He had no formal
schooling but learned the printing trade at a young age. Hearing of the Gold
Rush and opportunities in California, Bigler moved west to Sacramento,
where he practiced law and entered politics as a Democrat. He was elected
governor of California in 1852. Wanting to secure the miners' vote in the
next election, Bigler declared his first priority would be to protect the state's
profitable mining interests from monopolies and Chinese "coolies," whose
overwhelming numbers and servile status endangered the welfare of
California, a free state. A few days after his speech, miners in Tuolumne
County drafted resolutions to expel Chinese from the mines.*

EXECUTIVE DEPARTMENT,
Sacramento City, April 23d, 1852.

To the Senate and Assembly of the State of California:
   . . . The subject which I deem it my duty to present for your consideration before our final separation, is the present wholesale importation

*Journal of the Third Session of the Legislature of the State of California, Jan. 5, 1852–May 4,
1852 in Vallejo and Sacramento* (San Francisco: 1852), 373–78.

38

to this country of immigrants from the Asiatic quarter of the globe. I am deeply impressed with the conviction that, in order to enhance the prosperity and to preserve the tranquility of the State, measures must be adopted to check this tide of Asiatic immigration, and to prevent the exportation by them of the precious metal which they dig up from our soil without charge and without assuming any of the obligations imposed upon citizens. I allude particularly to a class of Asiatics known as "Coolies," who are sent here, as I am assured, and as is generally believed, under contracts to work in our mines for a term; and who, at the expiration of the term, return to their native country.[1] I am sensible that a proposition to restrict international intercourse, or to check the immigration of even Asiatics, would appear to conflict with the long cherished and benevolent policy of our Government. That Government has opened its paternal arms to "the oppressed of all nations," and it has offered them an asylum and a shelter from the iron rigor of despotism. The exile pilgrim and the weary immigrant have been the recipient of its noble hospitalities. In this generous policy, so far as it effects Europeans or others capable of becoming citizens under our laws, I desire to see no change; nor do I desire to see any diminution of that spirit of liberality which pervades the naturalization laws of the United States.

A question around which there has been thrown some doubt, is whether Asiatics could, with safety be admitted to the enjoyment of all the rights of citizens in our courts of justice. If they are ignorant of the solemn character of the oath or affirmation in the form prescribed by the Constitution and statutes, or if they are indifferent to the solemn obligation which an oath imposes to speak the truth, it would be unwise to receive them as jurors, or to permit them to testify in courts of law, more especially in cases affecting the rights of others than Asiatics.[2]

---

[1] The term "coolie" in Chinese means "unskilled laborer for hire." Used in conjunction with the "coolie trade," it refers to Chinese contract laborers who were brought to Cuba, Peru, and British Guiana to work for a term of service at a fixed rate of wages. This second meaning of the term was widely used by anti-Chinese agitators like Bigler to characterize Chinese labor as unfree and unfair competition and thereby to justify their exclusion, despite assertions by local newspapers, religious leaders, and the Joint Select Committee of the State Legislature that Chinese laborers were not coming as coolies under contract but as voluntary immigrants.

[2] Two years later in 1854, the California Supreme Court ruled in *People v. Hall* that a Chinese person (along with "Indian" and "Negro") could not testify against a white person in a California court of law. The ruling effectively freed a white man who had been convicted for the murder of a Chinese miner based on the testimonies of three Chinese witnesses. It was declared unconstitutional and voided by the Civil Rights Act of 1870.

Congress, possessing the exclusive power to establish a uniform rule of naturalization, has enacted that "every alien, being *a free white person*, may become a citizen of the United States," by complying with certain conditions. Of the construction of this law, Chancellor Kent remarks, that "the Act of Congress confines the description of Aliens capable of naturalization to free white persons." "I presume," continues the learned writer, "that this excludes the inhabitants of Africa and their descendants; and it may become a question to what extent persons of mixed blood are excluded, and what shades and degrees of mixture of color disqualify an alien from application for the benefits of the act of naturalization. Perhaps there might be difficulties, also, as to the copper-colored natives of America, or the yellow or tawny races of the Asiatics; and it may well be doubted whether any of them are white persons within the purview of the law. It is the declared law of New York, South Carolina, Tennessee, and other States, that Indians are not citizens, but distinct tribes, living under the protection of the government, and consequently, they never can be made citizens under the act of Congress."[3]

It is certain that no Asiatic has yet applied for, or has received the benefits of this act. Indeed, I am not aware that a single subject of the Chinese Empire ever acquired a residence or a domicil in any of the States of the Union, except perhaps in this. In this State their habits have been migratory; and so far as I can learn, very few of them have evinced a disposition to acquire a domicil, or, as citizens, to identify themselves with the country. Gold, with a talismanic power, has overcome these national habits of reserve and non-intercourse which the Chinese and their neighbors have hitherto exhibited; and under the impulse which the discovery of the precious metals in California has given to their cupidity, vast numbers of them are immigrating hither, not, however, to avail themselves of the blessings of a free government. They do not seek our land as "the asylum for the oppressed of all nations." They have no desire (even if permitted by the Constitution and laws) to absolve themselves from allegiance to other powers, and, under the laws of the United States, become American citizens. They come to acquire a certain amount of the precious metals, and then return to their native country.

I invite your attention for a moment to results that may ensue, if by inaction we give further encouragement to the mania for immigration which pervades several of the Asiatic states, and which it may be

---

[3]The Naturalization Act of 1790 limited naturalization to immigrants who were free white persons of good character, thus excluding Native Americans, indentured servants, slaves, free blacks, and Asians. Blacks were granted citizenship rights after the Civil War, Native Americans in 1924, Chinese in 1943, and other Asians in 1952.

presumed, is being rapidly diffused throughout all continental Asia. The area of Asia is 17,865,000 English square miles, and the total population is computed by the best authorities at 375,230,000. The population of the Chinese Empire and dependent states alone is 168,000,000. It will be readily perceived that millions might be detached from such myriads without any perceptible diminution of the aggregate population; and that vast numbers may be induced, under contracts, to immigrate to a country which they are told contains inexhaustible mines of gold and silver. The facilities afforded them for immigration are rapidly increasing, and few vessels now enter our ports from Asiatic countries which are not crowded with these peculiar people. I have received intelligence from reliable sources that the average rate charged an Asiatic from China to California is forty dollars; that over two thousand of their number have arrived at San Francisco within the last few weeks; and that at least five thousand are now on their way hither. Letters from Canton to the end of January, estimate the immigration from that port to California, for 1852 at over twenty thousand, nearly all of whom will be hired by Chinese masters, to come here and collect gold under the direction and control of the master himself, who accompanies them or of an agent. They usually come in bands of thirty or more; a vessel, however, recently arrived with one hundred on board, the whole being under the control of one man. A practice has long existed in China of hiring Coolies under contracts made there to work for a term of years in other countries. These Coolies are given a free passage out and home, with wages at the rate of $3 to $4 per month. Most of them are married, and, while absent, $1.50 to $2 per month is paid to their families for subsistence, and the amount deducted from their wages. The usual pay of Coolies employed as farmers in China, is $1 per month, and food enough to sustain life; but they are required to purchase their own clothing. . . .

If it be admitted that the introduction of one hundred thousand, or a less number of "Coolies," into this State, under such contracts with non-residents, may endanger the public tranquility and injuriously affect the interests of our people, then we are bound to adopt measures to avert such evils. I therefore respectfully submit for your consideration two distinct propositions:

1st. Such an exercise of the taxing power by the State as will check the present system of indiscriminate and unlimited Asiatic immigration.

2d. A demand by the State of California for the prompt interposition of Congress, by the passage of an Act prohibiting "Coolies," shipped to California under contracts, from laboring in the mines of this State. With the consent of the State, Congress would have the clear right to interpose such safeguards as in their wisdom might be deemed necessary. The power to tax as well as to entirely exclude this class of Asiatic immigrants, it is believed, can be constitutionally exercised by the State. . . .[4]

There is no official information in this Department touching the nature of the contracts said to have been made with Asiatics by their own countrymen, or by foreign residents in the Chinese Empire, to work in our mines. It is not officially known to this Department whether those persons are here in a state of voluntary or involuntary servitude. But if it be ascertained that their immigration and servitude is voluntary, I am still of the opinion that the Legislature may enact laws to prevent or discourage shipments of vast bodies of Coolies into this State. I am convinced not only that such a measure is necessary, but I am also convinced that there is nothing in the Federal Constitution which forbids the enactment of such laws.

It is a remarkable fact that the treaty concluded at Wang Hiya, on the 3d of July, 1845, between the United States and China, contains no provisions in relation to the civil or political privileges which the subjects of the Chinese Empire, immigrating to the United States, shall enjoy. It is true that this treaty guarantees important commercial privileges to our citizens; but in the exercise of these privileges, no encroachments are made upon the rights or the property of the subjects of China.[5] The measures which I have now recommended you to enact, would not, of course, justify any retaliation by Chinese upon Americans now residing in that country. Indeed, in view of the fact that in all the governments of Europe and Asia, foreigners are excluded from mines, and in view of the further fact that in those countries the precious metals are commonly retained by the government, to the exclusion even of their own citizens, it is not easy to believe that the Chinese will urge objections to the measures which I have here presented, if adopted.

It must be conceded that the extraordinary wants of this State will demand novel if not extraordinary legislation. The history and condition of California is peculiar—it is without parallel. Her resources, like her exigencies, are without precedent. In framing laws, therefore, to meet such exigencies, it is clear that we cannot be guided entirely

[4]Later, Congress would pass the Prohibition of Coolie Trade Act of 1862 and the Alien Contract Labor Law of 1885 to prohibit American vessels and U.S. residents from importing Chinese coolies or contract laborers.

[5]Signed on July 3, 1844, the Treaty of Wangxia granted the United States "most favored nation" status, resulting in the U.S. receiving the same commercial benefits as other powers such as Britain. No mention was made about guaranteeing the personal safety and equal rights of Chinese subjects in the United States until the Burlingame Treaty of 1868.

by precedents which have been established in the common course of events in other States. But, though our condition may sometimes require departures from precedents in the enactment, as well as in the execution of laws, we should not fail to follow the Constitution, both as our chart and as the palladium of our liberties.

Having thus performed one of the most important duties which will perhaps devolve upon me during my term of office, I commit this subject to your care, and entreat for it your careful consideration.

JOHN BIGLER

2

NORMAN ASING

To His Excellency Governor Bigler

May 5, 1852

Ten days after Governor Bigler's "Special Message" was published in the Daily Alta, *the following rejoinder by Norman Asing (aka Yuan Sheng) appeared in the same newspaper. Hailing from Xiangshan District in Guangdong Province, Asing left home in 1820, possibly as a sailor, and traveled to Europe and America. He settled in Charleston, South Carolina, where he became a merchant, Christian, and naturalized citizen. Upon return to China for a brief stay, Asing got wind of the California Gold Rush and decided to set sail for San Francisco on May 6, 1849. The City Directory listed him as proprietor of the Macao Wosung Restaurant in 1850 and as foreign consul in 1854. While some newspaper accounts depict him as an eloquent spokesman who identified fully with his newly adopted country, other accounts attest to his belligerency and ruthlessness in controlling illicit activities in the Chinese community. Nothing more was heard about Norman Asing after the 1860s.*

Sir:—I am a Chinaman, a republican, and a lover of free institutions; am much attached to the principles of the Government of the United States, and therefore take the liberty of addressing you as the chief of the Government of this State. Your official position gives you a great opportunity of good or evil. Your opinions through a message to a legislative body have weight, and perhaps none more so with the people, for the effects of your late message has been thus far to prejudice the public mind against my people, to enable those who wait the opportunity to hunt them down, and rob them of the rewards of their toil. You may not have meant that this should be the case, but you can see what will be the result of your propositions.

I am not much acquainted with your logic, that by excluding population from this State you enhance its wealth. I have always considered that population was wealth; particularly a population of producers, of men who by the labor of their hands or intellect, enrich the warehouses or the granaries of the country with the products of nature and art. You are deeply convinced you say "that to enhance the prosperity and to preserve the tranquility of this State, Asiatic immigration must be checked." This, your Excellency, is but one step towards a retrograde movement of the Government, which, on reflection, you will discover; and which the citizens of this country ought never to tolerate. It was one of the principal causes of quarrel between you (when colonies) and England; when the latter pressed laws against emigration, you looked for immigration; it came, and immigration made *you what you are*—your nation what it is. It transferred you at once from childhood to manhood and made you great and respectable throughout the nations of the earth. I am sure your Excellency cannot, if you would, prevent your being called the descendant of an immigrant, for I am sure you do not boast of being a descendant of the red man. But your further logic is more reprehensible. You argue that this is a republic of a particular race—that the constitution of the United States admits of no asylum to any other than the pale face. This proposition is false in the extreme, and you know it. The declaration of your independence, and all the acts of your government, your people, and your history are all against you.

It is true, you have degraded the negro because of your holding him in involuntary servitude, and because for the sake of union in some of your States such was tolerated, and amongst this class you would endeavor to place us; and no doubt it would be pleasing to some would-be freemen to mark the brand of servitude upon us. But we would beg to remind you that when your nation was a wilderness, and the nation from whom you sprung *barbarous*, we exercised most of the arts and virtues of civilized life; that we are possessed of a language and literature, and that men skilled in science and the arts are numerous among us; that the productions of our manufactories, our sail, and workshops, form no small share of the commerce of the world; and that for centuries, colleges, schools, charitable institutions, asylums and hospitals, have been as common as in your own land. That our people cannot be reproved for their idleness, and that your historians have given them due credit for the variety and richness of their works of art, and for their simplicity of manners, and particularly their industry. And we beg to remark, that so far as the history of our race in California goes, it stamps with the test of truth the fact that we are not the degraded race you would make us. We came amongst you as mechanics or traders, and following every honorable business of life. You do not find us pursuing occupations of a degrading character, except you consider labor degrading, which I am sure you do not; and if our countrymen save the proceeds of their industry from the tavern and the gambling house, to spend it in the purchase of farms or town lots or on their families, surely you will admit that even these are virtues. You say "you desire to see no change in the generous policy of this Government as far as regards Europeans." It is out of your power to say, however, in what way or to whom the doctrines of the Constitution shall apply. You have no more right to propose a measure for checking immigration, than you have the right of sending a message to the Legislature on the subject. As far as regards the color and complexion of our race, we are perfectly aware that our population have been a little more tanned than yours.

Your Excellency will discover, however, that we are as much allied to the *African* race or the red man as you are yourself, and that as far as the aristocracy of *skin is* concerned, ours might compare with many of the European races; nor do we consider that your Excellency, as a Democrat, will make us believe that the framers of your declaration of rights ever suggested the propriety of establishing an aristocracy of *skin.* I am a naturalized citizen,[1] your Excellency, of Charleston, South Carolina, and a Christian, too; and so hope you will stand corrected in your assertion "that none of the Asiatic class," as you are pleased to term them, "have applied for benefits under our naturalization act." I could point out to you numbers of citizens, all over the whole continent, who have taken advantage of your hospitality and citizenship, and I defy you to say that our race have ever abused that hospitality or forfeited

---

[1]Although the 1790 Naturalization Law limited naturalization to "free white persons," Norman Asing may have well been a naturalized citizen, as some state courts were willing to naturalize Chinese—a practice that was halted by Section 14 of the Chinese Exclusion Act.

their claim on this or any of the governments of South America, by an infringement on the laws of the countries into which they pass. You find us peculiarly peaceable and orderly. It does not cost your State much for our criminal prosecution. We apply less to your courts for redress, and so far as I know, there are none that are a charge upon the State as paupers.

You say that "gold, with its talismanic power, has overcome those natural habits of non-intercourse we have exhibited." I ask you, has not gold had the same effect upon your people, and the people of other countries, who have migrated hither? Why, it was gold that filled your country (formerly a desert) with people, filled your harbors with ships, and opened our much-coveted trade to the enterprise of your merchants.

You cannot, in the face of facts that stare you in the face, assert that the cupidity of which you speak is ours alone; so that your Excellency will perceive that in this age a change of cupidity would not tell. Thousands of your own citizens come here to dig gold, with the idea of returning as speedily as they can.

We think you are in error, however, in this respect, as many of us, and many more, will acquire a domicile amongst you.

But, for the present, I shall take leave of your Excellency, and shall resume this question upon another occasion, which I hope you will take into consideration in a spirit of candor. Your predecessor pursued a different line of conduct towards us, as will appear by reference to his message.[2]

I have the honor to be your Excellency's very obedient servant.

NORMAN ASING

---

[2]In his address to the California legislature in 1852, Governor John McDougal called the Chinese "one of the most worthy of our newly-adopted citizens" and recommended the use of land grants to encourage their further immigration and settlement in California.

3

FRANK PIXLEY

An Address to the People of California in Mass Meeting Assembled

April 5, 1876

On April 5, 1876, after the Republican Party had been overthrown in California's elections and with the presidential campaign underway, Democrats called for a mass meeting in San Francisco to consider their solution to the "evils of Chinese immigration." As reported in the San Francisco Chronicle, *the Union Hall was packed with 25,000 people from "all classes of society," and the streets surrounding the hall overflowed with people. Fifteen prominent citizens, the majority of them Democrats—including the mayor of San Francisco and the governor of California—spoke before attorney and politician Frank Pixley, representing the Committee of Citizens appointed by the San Francisco Board of Supervisors to investigate the Chinese problem, read the following report and proposed resolutions for Chinese exclusion. "The reading was frequently interrupted with applause," according to the* Chronicle, *"and at the conclusion the question was put on their adoption and carried with great acclaim." Pixley was a native of New York and had arrived in California on mule back during the Gold Rush. After spending two winters mining for gold, he entered politics as a Republican. He was elected to the State Assembly in 1858 and as attorney general of California in 1861.*

In considering the question of Chinese emigration the Committee are impressed with its importance as a local measure affecting the immediate interests of this coast, and as a national question involving important considerations for the future of the whole country.

The Committee bear in mind the history of the treaty legislation and the commercial considerations that have led to the present condition of affairs, and are not unmindful of the fact that our Chinese population have been invited to the country by the policy of our laws and the sanction of

"Anti-Chinese," *San Francisco Chronicle*, April 6, 1876.

our highest legislative and judicial tribunals; hence the Committee deem it proper to declare their intention to respect the provision of treaties, the decision of Courts and the higher considerations of humanity in dealing with those Chinese who are now domiciled in our midst.

The Committee recognize the General Government and its Congress as the only authority to which the people of this coast may look for the arrest of an emigration which, after so many years, has been demonstrated to be an evil of present and increasing magnitude. . . .

The Committee would call attention to the peculiar facts that have contributed to the speedy settlement of California.

Its gold and silver discoveries; its attractive climate; its very distinctive and wonderful resources. Also to the fact that China has not allowed emigration from its Empire till within the period of the American occupation of California; that this emigration has been impeded by such laws as California and San Francisco have from time to time attempted; that it is in defiance of Chinese traditions and embarrassed by religious and superstitious beliefs, and yet, with all these hindrances, the Chinese are one-fourth of our population, and are now coming to us in largely increasing numbers.

The Committee, considering the source from which we desire white emigration, and the source from whence comes the Chinese, forty million (40,000,000) in America against four hundred million (400,000,000) in Asia, considering also that this is an age of cheap transportation by reason of steam, considering the attractions of our country, its high price of labor, its protection to life and property, its splendid future prospects, in contrast with the prices of labor, the indifference to life and the inability to obtain or enjoy property in the overcrowded Empire of China, feel alarmed at this increasing invasion, and feel justified in calling the nation's attention to an evil of vast proportion which is now threatening to outnumber our Pacific Coast population, and imperil the best interests of this side of our continent.[1]

Against the heresy of cheap labor the Committee raises its protest.

Against the argument that Chinese labor is necessary to this coast it pronounces an unqualified denial.

The Committee rests its conclusions upon the fact that Chinese are not and never can become homogeneous; they are of distinct race, of a different and peculiar civilization; they do not speak our language, do

[1]Nativists often used the fear of a Chinese invasion of immigrants as a justification for Chinese exclusion. It never materialized. The Chinese population in the United States peaked at 107,488 in 1890—less than 1 percent of the nation's population and 9 percent of California's population.

not adopt our manners, customs or habits; are Pagan in belief; in contempt of our tribunals they establish secret ones of their own, enforce their secret laws in our midst, even to the penalty of death.

They fill our prisons, asylums and hospitals; are a grievous burden to our taxpayers; they cannot be used for the performance of military of civil duties; they can neither become soldiers nor sailors, jurors nor conservators of the peace; they will not conform in their habits of life to our sanitary or police regulations.

Their diseases are infectious and horrible; their vices are the result of (4000) years of practice. They buy and sell women for prostitution; they import peons and hold them to service against the spirit of our law by the enforcement of their secret tribunal. Without wives or homes, and by reason of their ability to dwell in crowded tenements, to live upon rice, tea, dried fish and desiccated vegetables, they can subsist more cheaply than white laborers who have families to support, children to educate, houses to maintain, taxes to pay and public duties to perform. Hence in the labor market the Chinese can under-bid the white man or woman. The contest is altogether unequal; and wherever it has been waged the Chinese have conquered, and the whites have been driven from employment. . . .

The Committee advise patience, moderation and cool counsel.

It recommends the sending to Washington of a delegation who shall intelligently and truthfully represent this question to our authorities at the National Capital; who shall be able to present all the facts touching the question, and to direct to its consideration the serious attention of our statements.

If Chinese emigration is an evil, there must of necessity be found a remedy. If existing treaties are found to work an injury to our people, they can be abrogated and another compact be entered into without sacrificing the good name or honor of the Government.

If the interest of the two people conflict, those of the Chinese must give way. If Oriental trade cannot be had except at the expense of the happiness and welfare of the American people, we must relinquish it. . . . In conclusion, we say to you, our fellow-citizens, and through you to the national authorities at Washington, that it is better to look to Congress for a peaceable and legal solution of this Chinese problem than to seek to precipitate or embarrass it by any effort of our own, outside of our local authorities in the firm administrations of our existing municipal law; therefore,

Resolved, That the sentiments embodied in the foregoing address, are expressions of the opinion of this assemblage, and in view of the facts therein set forth we earnestly recommend the Congress of the United States to give this matter of Chinese emigration its immediate and earnest attention.

Resolved, That the people of California, in their perfect loyalty to the Government and the law, recognize their duty to the Chinese now among us, promising them protection and all their rights, and a guarantee of all the privileges to which they are entitled under existing laws.

Resolved, That in relation to the continuing emigration of China, we claim the right, from our superior knowledge of the results of this emigration and our observation of its practical workings, and as an intelligent part of the American people, to declare our unalterable hostility to it, to say that the bulk of this emigration is pure and simple peonage.

Resolved, That the majority of the emigrants are coolies, in bondage to secret organizations more powerful than our Courts, and held in servitude for debt—a slavery only terminable at the will of masters, over whom our laws have no control.

Resolved, That this system is immoral and brutalizing—worse than African slavery. It involves a systematic violation of our State and municipal laws, and is attended by murder, subordination, kidnapping, and the sale of women for the purpose of prostitution.

Resolved, That the presence of these people in our midst has a tendency to demoralize society and minister to its worst vices; it aids to corrupt and debauch our youth, and the labor of this servile class comes in direct competition with the labor of American citizens. It degrades industrial occupation, drives white labor from the market, multiplies idlers and paupers, and is a menace to Christian civilization. If these things be true—and we challenge their successful denial—then we have a right to demand of Congress that it shall investigate, and then legislate for the abatement of this evil; therefore,

Resolved, That the General Committee having this meeting in charge shall appoint the Mayor of the city, appointing not to exceed five citizens of San Francisco, intelligent upon this Chinese question, who shall proceed to Washington, and, having submitted this address and these resolutions to the House of Congress, shall earnestly urge such legislation as may be necessary to meet the requirements of this occasion.

4

REPRESENTATIVE CHINAMEN IN AMERICA

A Memorial to His Excellency U. S. Grant, President of the United States

1876

The Chinese Six Companies, consisting of six district associations—members emigrated from the same districts in China—first formed in 1862. It looked after the interests of Chinese immigrants in the San Francisco region by settling disputes between district associations, defending Chinese against racial discrimination and violence, establishing public institutions like hospitals and schools, and eradicating prostitution. In 1882, the Chinese Six Companies formally united as the Chinese Consolidated Benevolent Association. The following memorial to President Grant, sent soon after the anti-Chinese rally on April 5, 1876, was one of many actions taken by the community organization to defend the reputation of Chinese immigrants against false accusations and to protest their mistreatment in American society.

Sir: In the absence of any Consular representative, we, the undersigned, in the name and in behalf of the Chinese people now in America, would most respectfully present for your consideration the following statements regarding the subject of Chinese emigration to this country.

I. We understand that it has always been the settled policy of your Honorable Government to welcome emigration to your shores from all countries, without let or hindrance.

The Chinese are not the only people who have crossed the ocean to seek a residence in this land.

II. The Treaty of Amity and Peace between the United States and China makes special mention of the rights and privileges of Americans in China, and also of the rights and privileges of Chinese in America.

Augustus Layres, *The Other Side of the Chinese Question with a Memorial to the President of the U.S. from Representative Chinamen in America* (San Francisco: Taylor and News, 1876), 20–24.

III. American steamers, subsidized by your Honorable Government, have visited the ports of China, and invited our people to come to this country to find employment and improve their condition. Our people have been coming to this country for the last twenty-five years, but up to the present time there are only 150,000 Chinese in all these United States, 60,000 of whom are in California, and 30,000 in the city of San Francisco.

IV. Our people in this country, for the most part, have been peaceable, law abiding, and industrious. They performed the largest part of the unskilled labor in the construction of the Central Pacific Railroad, and also of all other railroads on this Coast. They have found useful and remunerative employment in all the manufacturing establishments of this coast, in agricultural pursuits, and in family service. While benefiting themselves with the honest reward of their daily toil, they have given satisfaction to their employers, and have left all the results of their industry to enrich the State. They have not displaced white laborers from these positions, but have simply multiplied the industrial enterprises of the country.

V. The Chinese have neither attempted nor desired to interfere with the established order of things in this country, either of politics or religion. They have opened no whiskey saloons, for the purpose of dealing out poison and degrading their fellow men. They have promptly paid their duties, their taxes, their rents, and their debts.

VI. It has often occurred, about the time of the State and general elections, that political agitators have stirred up the minds of the people in hostility to the Chinese, but formerly the hostility has usually subsided after the elections were over.

VII. At the present time an intense excitement and bitter hostility against the Chinese in this land, and against further Chinese immigration, has been created in the minds of the people, led on by His Honor the Mayor of San Francisco, and his associates in office, and approved by His Excellency the Governor, and other great men of the State.

These great men gathered some 20,000 of the people of this city together on the evening of April the fifth, and adopted an address and resolutions against Chinese immigration. They have since appointed three men (one of whom we understand to be the author of the address and resolutions[1]) to carry that address and those resolutions to your

---

[1]Frank Pixley was a journalist, attorney, and former attorney general of California. He reported on the findings and resolutions of the Committee of Citizens at the mass meeting and would play a major role in the hearings of the Senate Joint Special Committee to investigate Chinese immigration in the following months.

Excellency, and to present further objections, if possible, against the immigration of the Chinese to this country.

VIII. In that address numerous charges are made against our people, some of which are highly colored and sensational, and others, having no foundation whatever in fact, are only calculated to mislead honest minds and create an unjust prejudice against us.

We wish most respectfully to call your attention, and, through you, the attention of Congress, to some of the statements of that remarkable paper, and ask a careful comparison of the statements there made with the facts of the case; and

(a) It is charged against us that not one virtuous Chinawoman has been brought to this country, and that here we have no wives nor children.

The fact is, that already a few hundred Chinese families have been brought here. These are all chaste, pure, keepers-at-home, not known on the public street. There are also among us a few hundred, perhaps a thousand, Chinese children born in America.

The reason why so few of our families are brought to this country is because it is contrary to the custom, and against the inclination of virtuous Chinese women to go so far from home, and because the frequent outbursts of popular indignation against our people have not encouraged us to bring our families with us against their will.

Quite a number of Chinese prostitutes have been brought to this country by unprincipled Chinamen, but these, at first, were brought from China at the instigation, and for the gratification of white men. And even at the present time, it is commonly reported that a part of the proceeds of this villainous traffic goes to enrich a certain class of men belonging to this Honorable nation — a class of men, too, who are under solemn obligation to suppress the whole vile business, and who certainly have it in their power to suppress it, if they so desired.

A few years ago our Chinese merchants tried to send these prostitutes back to China, and succeeded in getting a large number on board the out-going steamer; but a certain lawyer of your Honorable nation, (said to be the author and bearer of these resolutions against our people,) in the employ of unprincipled Chinamen, procured a writ of "habeas corpus," and brought all those women on shore again, and the Courts decided that they had a right to stay in this country if they so desired. Those women are still here, and the only remedy for this evil and also for the evil of Chinese gambling lies, so far as we can see, in an honest and impartial administration of Municipal Government in all its details, even including the police department. If officers would refuse bribes, then unprincipled Chinamen could no longer purchase immunity from the punishment of their crimes.

(b) It is charged against us that we have purchased no real estate. The general tone of public sentiment has not been such as to encourage us to invest in real estate, and yet our people have purchased and now own over $800,000 worth of real estate in San Francisco alone.

(c) It is charged against us that we eat rice, fish, and vegetables. It is true that our diet is slightly different from the people of this Honorable country; our tastes in these matters are not exactly alike and cannot be forced. But is that a sin on our part, of sufficient gravity to be brought before the President and Congress of the United States?

(d) It is charged that the Chinese are no benefit to this country. Are the railroads built by Chinese labor no benefit to the country? Are the manufacturing establishments, largely worked by Chinese labor, no benefit to this country? Do not the results of the daily toil of a hundred thousand men increase the riches of this country? Is it no benefit to this country that the Chinese annually pay over $2,000,000 duties at the Custom House of San Francisco? Is not the $200,000 annual poll tax paid by the Chinese any benefit? And are not the hundreds of thousands of dollars taxes on personal property, and the Foreign Miners' tax, annually paid to the revenues of this country, any benefit?

(e) It is charged against us that the "Six Chinese Companies" have secretly established judicial tribunals, jails and prisons, and secretly exercise judicial authority over the people. This charge has no foundation in fact. These Six Companies were originally organized for that purpose of mutual protection and care of our people coming to and going from this country. The Six Companies do not claim, nor do they exercise any judicial authority whatever, but are the same as any tradesmen or protective and benevolent societies. If it were true that the Six Companies exercise judicial authority over the Chinese people, then why do all the Chinese people still go to American Tribunals to adjust their differences, or to secure the punishment of their criminals?

Neither do these Companies import either men or women into this country.

(f) It is charged that all Chinese laboring men are slaves. This is not true in a single instance. Chinamen labor for bread. They pursue all kinds of industries for a livelihood.

Is it so then that every man laboring for his livelihood is a slave? If these men are slaves, then all men laboring for wages are slaves.

(g) It is charged that the Chinese commerce brings no benefit to American Bankers and Importers. But the fact is that an immense trade is carried on between China and the United States by American merchants, and all the carrying business of both countries, whether by steamers, sailing vessels or railroad, is done by Americans. No China ships are engaged in the carrying traffic between the two countries.

Is it a sin to be charged against us that the Chinese merchants are able to conduct their mercantile business on their own capital? And is not the exchange of millions of dollars annually by the Chinese with the banks of this city any benefit to the banks?

(h) We respectfully ask a careful consideration of all the foregoing statements. The Chinese are not the only people, nor do they bring the only evils that now afflict this country. And since the Chinese people are now here under solemn treaty rights, we hope to be protected according to the terms of this treaty.

But, if the Chinese are considered detrimental to the best interests of this country, and if our presence here is offensive to the American people, let there be a modification of existing treaty relations between China and the United States, either prohibiting or limiting further Chinese immigration, and, if desirable, requiring also the gradual retirement of the Chinese people, now here, from this country. Such an arrangement, though not without embarrassments to both parties, we believe, would not be altogether unacceptable to the Chinese Government, and, doubtless, it would be very acceptable to a certain class of people in this Honorable country.

With sentiments of profound respect,

Lee Ming How, *President Sam Yup Company.*
Lee Chee Kwan, *President Yung Wo Company.*
Law Yee Chung, *President Kong Chow Company.*
Chan Leung Kok, *President Ning Yung Company.*
Lee Cheong Chip, *President Hop Wo Company.*
Chan Kong Chew, *President Yan Wo Company.*
Lee Tong Hay, *President Chinese Young Men's Christian Association.*

5

THE TIMES

The Wild Hoodlum: Kearney's Visit to Philadelphia

August 31, 1878

Denis Kearney, an Irish Catholic labor agitator, is best known for leading the anti-Chinese movement as a crusade for the white working class and for coining the motto, "The Chinese must go!" Born in Ireland, Kearney went to sea as a cabin boy at eleven and arrived in San Francisco in 1868, where he got married, established a draying business, and became a U.S. citizen. In 1877, at the height of the Long Depression, he founded the Workingmen's Party of California and spoke out against land monopolies, corrupt politicians, and Chinese labor in the sandlots near City Hall. Kearney's dramatic oratorical style and incendiary language attracted large, diverse crowds of people, and he was arrested a number of times for inciting violence.

As president of the Workingmen's Party, Kearney attempted to organize white laborers across the country. In 1878 he went on a four-month speaker's tour, but his "vulgar rhetoric and lack of argument" met with mixed reviews from workers and labor leaders in the East. The following excerpts from a newspaper article in the Times *(of Philadelphia) provide a detailed description of Denis Kearney's appearance, oratorical style, and anti-Chinese rhetoric as he delivered a speech to a crowd of 5,000 in the open space of an old Mansion House in Philadelphia.*

Kearney appears to be about 35 years of age, or probably a twelvemonth or so less. Standing, his height reaches five feet seven inches. Broad shoulders, closely knit frame, straight up and down under-pinning, and feet of average proportions. The head is a large one, and round as an apple. . . . The forehead is broad and low, with two great seams running across from temple to temple. The eyes, as seen in the dim light of the car, dark, small and shifty. High cheek bones surround a full and rather

"The Wild Hoodlum: Kearney's Visit to Philadelphia," *The Times*, August 31, 1878, 1.

squatty nose, beneath which a short sandy moustache does not hide from view a goodly sized mouth, overtopping a square, heavy jaw. The head of the great agitator rests upon a bull neck, and his complexion is that of the average seaside sojourner. His hands are small and shapely and give little token of having performed any great amount of manual labor at any recent date. Kearney was dressed in a $14 blue flannel suit, wore a calico shirt and lie-down collar, and had on a black and white silk necktie, tied with a sailor knot. His big black Buffalo Bill hat was resting over his head. . . .

KEARNEY'S STYLE OF DELIVERY

But he is very far from being an orator. He is not eloquent and there is not the slightest touch of magnetism in his voice. He has a parcel of rounded phrases and high-sounding invectives and these he hurled at an audience the half of which did not know the meaning of his words. But they laughed at them and thought the speech a mighty fine one. Kearney has the slightest touch of the Irish brogue. He is rich in gesture of a certain kind. He swings his arms around him and then, when inveighing against the "lecherous bondholders"—he still clings to that woefully and wonderfully misapplied adjective—or the "slimy imps of hell," or some such rascals, he clutches his white, delicately-moulded hands, making fists that are far from horny, and shakes them menacingly at the characters he had conjured up. He speaks earnestly, but his speech last night was not an impromptu affair. In fact, it appeared to be the same effort that East and West have listened to, and that it was written for Denis was shown by the fact that after every interruption he went back several sentences in his speech and repeated them over again verbatim. Last night's talk was more devoid of blasphemy than any of the speeches thus far credited to the California agitator, but at one point—in his reference to the "leprous" Chinaman—he gave an incident and elaborated upon it in a way so nasty as to render it unfit for publication. "I'm going to use the English language," he said, as though in apology, "as I understand it, and not as some Bohemian ghoul understands it." . . .

SOME TALK ABOUT ALMOND EYES

My friends, I beg your indulgence. You see that I am not able to speak. I have just given you a disjointed affair. I am tired, weak and feeble. I am not nearly as strong as I was six months ago. But I cannot close my argument without giving a description about the almond-eyed, leprous, long-tailed parasite that infests the State of California. I know there are Californians within the sound of my voice. They know all about the Chinese lepers of California. I have advices from there two days ago that no less than seven lepers were found by the Board of Health in visiting Chinatown last week; and they only visited three different places, and they found five lepers in one house, and yesterday one of our delegates to the Constitutional Convention, in searching for leperous Chinamen, found leperous Chinamen washing and ironing clothing for some fashionable young lady. [Applause.] The speaker's remarks at this point were too vulgar and obscene for publication. He then went on: These Chinamen in California work night and day. They work for a dollar a day and board themselves, and if a white man offered to work for a dollar they would work for ninety cents, and so on. They will reduce their pay, if forced to, to twenty cents a day. They live and make money at twenty cents a day and keep their country cousins besides. I tell you, friends, they work night and day in gangs. A gang of Chinamen will hire a room, or, rather, the Six Chinese Companies will hire a room for them, a room that one white man would want. They will divide that room into different apartments and stow the Chinamen in there, like sardines in boxes, heads and points. Then if one gang goes to work in a shop they leave another gang there. One gang occupies the room at night and another at day, and when they leave the shop they go back and occupy the same room that the other man left, and they keep on in that manner day after day, week after week and month after month, and send every dollar earned in the State of California to China, never to return. They buy nothing in this country. They are imported here as slaves by their superiors, they are mortgaged body and soul. They do with them as they please, and just as true as these men refuse to pay their per capita tax the secret tribunal of the Six Chinese Companies is set at work and they are hung and butchered and pitched into the street. This is an every-day occurrence in the State of California, but I find the Chinese are all over the United States. You have got some of them in Philadelphia. [Cries of "Too many."] But we in California are going to stop it. [Cries of "Good! Good! Hear! Hear!"] We have charge of the State of California and if we are compelled to drive the Chinamen out of California, if they don't leave of their free will when we give them ample notice to so leave, we shall do so. I tell you now that we are going to block up the Golden Gate of San Francisco with their festering carcasses, and we are going to fill up the crevices with the thieves that brought them to this country. [Applause.] I tell you the Anglo-Saxon or American freemen will not submit to be driven to the wall. [Cries of "Hear! Hear!"] Why, if we are forced to compete with the above class of laboring slaves what is to become of us? What is to become of this Republic? I ask and pause to reply. [A voice, "It will go to hell."] It is going to hell fast, and I tell you, friends, I see visions of an empire in the future. What do you suppose Grant has gone to Europe for? Already he has organized a dynasty. The workingmen of Washington are looking after him.[1] [At this point a man made a disturbance in front of the platform.] This man is all right; he is honest and enthusiastic; he is a workingman, and of course he is oppressed by the thieves of this country, and he must give vent to his feelings or else he will blow up. Friends, in conclusion, let me beg of you again to pool your issues and capture the State of Pennsylvania. You do that and then you will do your duty and take the first step to the emancipation of labor. [Cries, "How about Grant?"] Grant will come over here about 1880 and take charge of this country, but, I tell you, then he will find the workingmen in power—he will find the workingmen will have their pickets on duty, spread all over the country. Friends, we know that the other parties have been weighed in the balance and found wanting. Already the mutterings of the thunder that precedes the coming storm is heard on every hand. The handwriting is on the wall; even the leaves in the mighty forest are whispering to each other of a disintegration that is taking place, and when the workingmen of the United States will know their power, and rise in their majesty and their might and the tornado bursts over the land, then what will become of the false swearers, the perjured judges, the thieves that have fattened upon robbery and thrived upon corruption? They will be driven into outer darkness, and I say, may God have mercy upon their infernal souls. Now, in conclusion, I must appeal to your pockets to-night. I have got twenty-five cents left to go to Baltimore and I must appeal to the men to-night to take up a small collection here to pay my expenses to Baltimore and then to New Jersey. Will you do it? [Cries, "O, yes!"] I want this understood, friends, that I am working not for pay; I am not working for money, but my expenses must be paid. I can get plenty of thieves to pay my expenses and to pay me well, but I want none of their thieving lucre. I want none of their gold.

---

[1] In 1877, after serving two terms as president of the United States, Ulysses S. Grant embarked on a two-year world tour before returning to run for a third term in 1880, which he lost.

THE RESOLUTIONS

When Kearney had concluded the following resolutions were offered and adopted:

WHEREAS, This evening at the National Capital an American citizen, attempting to exercise his constitutional privilege of free speech, guaranteed by our fathers and the blood of our brethren, was struck by an officer of the national authority; and

WHEREAS, That American citizen, knowing his rights, dared maintain them in the face of the authority, was sustained by our fellow-citizens at Washington; therefore be it

RESOLVED, By the workingmen of Philadelphia, in mass meeting assembled to the number of forty thousand,[2] that we denounce in the most unmeasured terms the acts of the national authority on that occasion.

RESOLVED, That we demand that the proper authorities at Washington investigate the outrage to the end that the prime mover may be discovered and held up to the scorn of an outraged people.

RESOLVED, That we recognize Mr. Kearney's action on that occasion as one of the noblest examples of heroism in modern history and worthy of public recognition at the hands of a free people.[3]

RESOLVED, That we emphatically indorse the California workingmen's motto that "the Chinese must go."

[2]The reporter had gauged the crowd to be 5,000 while Denis Kearney had estimated it to be 20,000 earlier.

[3]A police captain tried to prevent Kearney from speaking at the Capitol the night before, but Kearney prevailed.

6

SENATORS JOHN F. MILLER
AND GEORGE FRISBIE HOAR

Congressional Debate on Chinese Exclusion
February 28–March 1, 1882

After President Hayes vetoed the Fifteen Passenger Bill for violating the terms of the Burlingame Treaty, Commissioner James B. Angell negotiated a new treaty with China in 1881, which allowed for restrictions but not prohibition of Chinese immigration. Congress was then ready to consider new legislation to implement the Angell Treaty. Debate over Senate Bill 71 began on February 28, 1882, with combatants Senator John F. Miller (R-CA) and Senator George Frisbie Hoar (R-MA) setting the tone and terms of the debate. A lawyer, businessman, and major general in the Union Army during the Civil War, Miller had been recently elected to the U.S. Senate after chairing the anti-Chinese committee at the California constitutional convention. Following Miller's speech, Senator Hoar spoke the next day against the bill. The proud grandson of Roger Sherman, one of the signers of the Declaration of Independence, Hoar was the Republican flag-bearer of workers' rights, women's suffrage, and racial equality. A seasoned statesman, he had represented Massachusetts since 1869.

After eight days of speeches by twenty senators with staunch support coming from Democrats as well as West Coast and Southern Republicans, Senate Bill 71 passed 29 to 15 (32 not voting), with 20 Democrats and 9 Republicans voting in favor, and 1 Democrat and 14 Republicans in opposition. Similar arguments were raised in the House as 70 Representatives debated the twenty-year exclusion bill for seven days. The bill passed 167 to 66 (59 not voting), with 107 Democrats and 60 Republicans in favor, and 4 Democrats and 62 Republicans in opposition. The Senate bill was sent to President Chester A. Arthur for approval. Believing that the legislation was too sweeping and a clear violation of the Angell Treaty, the president chose to veto the bill.

---

13 *Congressional Record*, 1482–1487 (February 28, 1882); 13 *Congressional Record*, 1515–1523 (March 1, 1882).

SENATOR JOHN F. MILLER

The political history of this country may be searched in vain for an example of such perfect unanimity of expression by the parties at any time contending for political power upon a question of governmental policy. It would seem that the question of Chinese restriction has passed the stage of argument. To such a policy both political parties are equally pledged, bound, and committed by the most solemn and deliberate acts and declarations, and if these declarations were made in earnest, this or a like measure will pass both houses nearly unanimously. The vote upon this bill will determine, I think, whether the leaders of the two great political parties of this country were in earnest in making these declarations, or whether they were made merely to deceive the people and to catch votes. . . .

It has been said that the advocates of Chinese restriction were to be found only among the vicious, unlettered, foreign element of California society. To show the fact in respect of this contention, the Legislature of California in 1878 provided for a vote of the people upon the question of Chinese immigration (so called) to be had at the general election of 1879. The vote was legally taken, without excitement, and the response was general. When the ballots were counted, there were found to be 883 votes for Chinese immigration and 154,638 against it. A similar vote was taken in Nevada and resulted as follows: 183 votes for Chinese immigration and 17,259 votes against it. It has been said that a count of noses is an ineffectual and illusory method of settling great questions, but the vote of those two states settled the contention intended to be settled; and demonstrated that the people of all others in the United States who know most of the Chinese evil, and who are most competent to judge of the necessity for restriction are practically unanimous in the support of this measure. . . .

It is a fact of history that wherever the Chinese have gone they have always taken their habits, methods, and civilization with them; and history fails to record a single example in which they have ever lost them. They remain Chinese always and everywhere; changeless, fixed, and unalterable. In this respect they differ from all other peoples who have come to our shores. The men of every other race or nation who go abroad, sooner or later, adopt the civilization of the people by whom they are surrounded, and assimilate with or are absorbed in the mass of humanity with which they come in constant contact. The Chinese are alone perfectly unimpressible, and even their offspring born on American soil and who have grown up surrounded by American influences are Chinese in every characteristic of mind, feature, form, habit, and method, precisely the same as their fathers and their ancestors in China. We have found that no impression has been or can be made upon the civilization which confronts ours on the Pacific coast. An "irrepressible conflict" is now upon us in full force, and those who do not see it in progress are not so wise as the men who saw the approach of that other "irrepressible conflict" which shook the very foundations of American empire upon this continent.

If we continue to permit the introduction of this strange people, with their peculiar civilization, until they form a considerable part of our population, what is to be the effect upon the American people and Anglo-Saxon civilization? Can these two civilizations endure side by side as two distinct and hostile forces? Can these two forces abide in such close relation without conflict? Is American civilization as unimpressible as Chinese civilization? When the end comes for one or the other, which will be found to have survived? Can they meet half way, and so merge in a mongrel race, half Chinese and half Caucasian, as to produce a civilization half pagan, half Christian, semi-oriental, altogether mixed and very bad?

I insist that these questions are practical, and must have answers. We have already seen in California that the American people are far more impressible than the stoical Chinese, and the influence of Chinese methods and practices upon the social economy and moral condition of our people is plainly visible. The presence of the Chinese has produced a labor system which is unique; at least different from that of any other part of the United States. This is seen in the wandering, unsettled habits of white farm laborers, who, forced into competition with the Chinese, have been compelled to adopt their nomadic habit. So that the white farm laborer in California has no home in the family he serves, as in these Eastern States, but he is a "blanket man," who works in the fields only during the planting and harvest seasons, roaming the remainder of the year in search of other employment, his shelter the straw stack, and his food anything he can get. Under this system the great wheat growers carry on immense operations without the necessity of employing continuous labor, and the result is, large farming, to the exclusion of small American homes.

The new element in American society called the "hoodlum" is the result of Chinese competition in the manufacturing districts in California, by which young people of both sexes are driven to idleness in the streets. Strange and incurable maladies, loathsome and infectious diseases have been introduced which no medical skill can circumscribe or extirpate, and the stupefying, destructive opium habit is steadily increasing among our people. These and many other evidences of the demoralizing influence of Chinese civilization are open to the dullest observation. It is said, however, that the Chinese do not come in sufficient numbers nor remain long enough in the country to disturb the equilibrium of American society, or threaten a change in American institutions or the adulteration of our civilization. Individual Chinese come and go. As a people they remain. The number of Chinese in the United States is increasing constantly from year to year, as steadily as the steamships come and go. . . .

During the late depression in business affairs, which existed for three or four years in California, while thousands of white men and women were walking the streets, begging and pleading for an opportunity to give their honest labor for any wages, the great steamers made their regular arrivals from China, and discharged at the wharves of San Francisco their accustomed cargoes of Chinese, who were conveyed through the city to the distributing dens of the Six Companies, and within three or four days after arrival every Chinaman was in his place at work, and the white people unemployed still went about the streets. This continued until the white laboring men rose in their desperation and threatened the existence of the Chinese colony, when the influx was temporarily checked; but now, since business has revived and the pressure is removed, the Chinese come in vastly increased numbers, the excess of arrivals over departures averaging about one thousand per month at San Francisco alone. The importers of Chinese find no difficulty in securing openings for their cargoes now, and when transportation from California to the Eastern States is cheapened, as it soon will be they will extend their operations into the Middle and Eastern States, unless prevented by law, for wherever there is a white man or woman at work for wages, whether at the shoe bench, in the factory, or on the farm, there is an opening for a Chinaman. No matter how low the wages may be, the Chinaman can afford to work for still lower wages, and if the competition is free, he will take the white man's place. . . .

I make this appeal in behalf of a grand people, generous, loyal, brave, enterprising, and intelligent. They are a part of the great American people; they are your brethren. They went out over the trackless plain, the dreary desert, or else sailed over stormy seas, from New England, from New York, from Ohio, from the great empire of the Northwest, from the sunny South, from every part of every State in this glorious Union of States. There, in the once far off land of California, they have made the conquest of nature. They are laying the foundations of empire there, and they are laying them strong and deep. They are forming and building up American institutions based on Anglo-Saxon civilization. They have seen and understand that there can be no stability to their institutions and government unless based upon one civilization. Government is the product of civilization. It is evolved from the civilization of the people who ordain it. Free government cannot be maintained permanently in any country in which there exist two diverse and antagonistic civilizations of nearly equal strength. They operate as antagonistic hostile forces, and one or the other must have the ascendency.

If the civilization of a people changes, the government must change to conform to it. In California Chinese civilization in its pure essence appears as a rival to American civilization. It is the product of a people alien in every characteristic to our people, and it has never yet produced and never can evolve any form of government other than an imperial despotism. Free government is incompatible with it, and both cannot exist together. We ask of you to secure to us American Anglo-Saxon civilization without contamination or adulteration with any other. We make our appeal within the spirit of the Constitution of the United States in its highest interpretation. Its framers declared that it was—"Ordained to establish justice, insure domestic tranquility, provide for the common defense, promote the general welfare, and secure the blessings of liberty to ourselves and our posterity."

In order to insure general tranquility, peace and good order must be secured to every part of the country; to provide for the common defense involves the protection of every part; to promote the general welfare, the rights and interests of every section must be guarded; to secure the blessings of liberty to ourselves and our posterity, our free republican government must be maintained and administered in every portion of our land, and made permanent by keeping pure and uncontaminated the progressive civilization which gives it life and being. If you ask me how we may best "insure domestic tranquility and promote the general welfare" on the Pacific coast, I answer by passing this bill and enforcing its provisions to the letter. China for the Chinese! California for Americans and those who will become Americans!

SENATOR GEORGE HOAR

Nothing is more in conflict with the genius of American institutions than legal distinctions between individuals based upon race or upon occupation. The framers of our Constitution believed in the safety and wisdom of adherence to abstract principles. They meant that their laws would make no distinction between men except such as were required by personal conduct and character. The prejudices of race, the last of human delusions to be overcome, has been found until lately in our constitutions and statutes, and has left its hideous and ineradicable stains on our history in crimes committed by every generation. The negro, the Irishman, and the Indian have in turn been its victims here, as the Jew and the Greek and the Hindoo in Europe and Asia. But it is reserved for us at the present day, for the first time, to put into the public law of the world and into the national legislation of the foremost of republican nations a distinction inflicting upon a large class of men a degradation by reason of their race and by reason of their occupation.

The bill which passed Congress two years ago and was vetoed by President Hayes, the treaty of 1881, and the bill now before the Senate, have the same origin and are parts of the same measure. Two years ago it was proposed to exclude Chinese laborers from our borders, in express disregard of our solemn treaty obligations. This measure was arrested by President Hayes. The treaty of 1881 extorted from unwilling China her consent that we might regulate, limit, or suspend the coming of Chinese laborers into this country — a consent of which it is proposed by this bill to take advantage. This is entitled "A bill to enforce treaty stipulations with China."

It seems necessary in discussing the statute briefly to review the history of the treaty. First let me say that the title of this bill is deceptive. There is no stipulation of the treaty which the bill enforces. The bill where it is not inconsistent with the compact only avails itself of a privilege which that concedes. China only relaxed the Burlingame treaty so far as to permit us to "regulate, limit, or suspend the coming or residence" of Chinese laborers, "but not absolutely to prohibit it." The treaty expressly declares "such limitation or suspension shall be reasonable." But here is proposed a statute which for twenty years, under the severest penalties, absolutely inhibits the coming of Chinese laborers to this country. The treaty pledges us not absolutely to prohibit it. The bill is intended absolutely to prohibit it. . . .

Here is a declaration made by a compact between the two greatest nations of the Pacific, and now to be re-enforced by a solemn act of legislation, which places in the public law of the world and in the jurisprudence of America the principle that it is fit that there should hereafter be a distinction in the treatment of men by governments and in the recognition of their rights to the pursuit of happiness by a peaceful change of their homes, based not on conduct, not on character, but upon race and upon occupation. You may justly deny to the Chinese what you may not justly deny to the Irishman. You may deny to the laborer what you may not deny to the scholar or to the idler. And this declaration is extorted from unwilling China by the demand of America. With paupers, lazzaroni, harlots, persons afflicted with pestilential diseases, laborers are henceforth to be classed in the enumerations of American public law.

Certainly, Mr. President, this is an interesting and important transaction. It is impossible to overstate or to calculate the consequences which are likely to spring from a declaration made by the United States limiting human rights, especially a declaration in a treaty which is to become the international law governing these two great nations. As my friend from California [Mr. Miller] well said, it is of the earth earthy. The United States within twenty years has taken its place as the chief power on the Pacific. Whatever rivalry or whatever superiority we may be compelled to submit to elsewhere, our advantage of position, unless the inferiority be in ourselves, must give us superiority there. Are we to hold out two faces to the world, one to Europe and another to Asia? Or are we to admit that the doctrine we have proclaimed so constantly for the first century of our history is a mere empty phrase or a lie?

For myself and for the State of Massachusetts, so far as it is my privilege to represent her, I refuse consent to this legislation. I will not consent to a denial by the United States of the right of every man who desires to improve his condition by honest labor—his labor being no man's property but his own—to go anywhere on the face of the earth that he pleases. . . .

The advocates of this legislation appeal to a twofold motive for its support.

First. They invoke the old race prejudice which has so often played its hateful and bloody part in history.

Second. They say that the Chinese laborer works cheap and lives cheap, and so injures the American laborer with whom he competes. . . .

An argument is based on the character of the Chinese. You should take a race at its best, and not at its worst, in looking for its possibilities under the influence of freedom. The Chinese are in many particulars far superior to our own ancestors as they were when they first came forth into the light of history. Our British forefathers, at a time far within the historic period, remained in a degradation of superstition and a degradation of barbarism to which China never descended. Centuries after the Chinese philosopher had uttered the golden rule, and had said, "I like life and I like righteousness; if I cannot keep the two together I will let life go; and choose righteousness," the Druids of Britain were offering human sacrifices to pagan deities. We must take a race at its best in determining its capacity for freedom. This race can furnish able merchants, skillful diplomatists, profound philosophers, faithful servants, industrious and docile laborers. An eminent member of the other House told me that he had dealt with Chinese merchants to the amount of hundreds of thousands, perhaps millions, and that they had never deceived him. . . .

But the Chinese, it is said, will not assimilate with us. It is said the two races have been side by side for thirty years and no step taken toward assimilation. It is admitted that they have learned our industries rapidly and intelligently. That they do not incline to become Christians or republicans may perhaps be accounted for by the treatment they have received. They are excluded by statute from the public schools. They have no honest trial by jury. . . .

But, Mr. President, what special inducements have the Chinese to become republicans in a State which has established a constitution which in article 2, section 1, says: No native of China . . . shall ever exercise the privileges of an elector in this State. . . . And in article 19, section 2: No corporation . . . shall, after the adoption of this constitution, employ, directly or indirectly, in any capacity, any Chinese or Mongolian. And in section 3, of the same article: No Chinese shall be employed on any State, county, municipal, or other public work, except in punishment for crime. Then in section 4, same article: The Legislature shall delegate all necessary power to the incorporated cities and towns of this state for the removal of Chinese without the limits of such cities and towns . . . and it shall also provide the necessary legislation to prohibit the introduction into this State of Chinese after the adoption of this constitution. . . .

But it is urged, and this, in my judgment, is the greatest argument for the bill, that the introduction of the labor of the Chinese reduces the wages of the American laborer. "We are ruined by Chinese cheap labor" is a cry not limited to the class to whose representative the brilliant humorist of California first ascribed it.[1] I am not in favor of lowering anywhere the wages of any American labor, skilled or unskilled. On the contrary, I believe the maintenance and the increase of the purchasing power of the wages of the American workingman should be the one principal object of our legislation. The share in the product of agriculture or manufacture which goes to labor should, and I believe will, steadily increase. For that, and for that only, exists our protective system. The

---

[1]Bret Harte, "Plain Language from Truthful James," *Overland Monthly*, September 1870, 287–88. See Document 8.

acquisition of wealth, national or individual, is to be desired only for that. The statement of the accomplished Senator from California on this point meets my heartiest concurrence. I have no sympathy with any men, if such there be, who favor high protection and cheap labor.

But I believe that the Chinese, to whom the terms of the California Senator attribute skill enough to displace the American in every field, requiring intellectual vigor, will learn very soon to insist on his full share of the product of his work. But whether that be true or not, the wealth he creates will make better and not worse the condition of every higher class of labor. There may be trouble or failure in adjusting new relations. But sooner or later every new class of industrious and productive laborers elevates the class it displaces. The dread of an injury to our labor from the Chinese rests on the same fallacy that opposed the introduction of labor-saving machinery, and which opposed the coming of the Irishman and the German and the Swede. With my memory in New England all the lower places in factories, all places of domestic service, were filled by the sons and daughters of American farmers. The Irishmen came over to take their places; but the American farmer's son and daughter did not suffer; they were only elevated to a higher plane. In the increased wealth of the community their share is much greater. The Irishman rose from the bog or the hovel of his native land to the comfort of a New England home and placed his children in a New England school. The Yankee rises from the loom and the spinning-jenny to be the teacher, the skilled laborer in the machine shop, the inventor, the merchant, or the opulent landholder and farmer of the West. . . .

California has a population of 700,000. She can support seventeen million. Will it be claimed that these seventeen million will not be better off by finding there the wealth and the improvements which Chinese labor will prepare for their possession; by finding the railroad built, the swamp drained, the highway smoothed, the harbor dredged? . . .

Humanity, capable of infinite depths of degradation, is capable also of infinite heights of excellence. The Chinese, like all other races, has given us its examples of both. To rescue humanity from this degradation is, we are taught to believe, the great object of God's moral government on earth. It is not by injustice, exclusion, caste, but by reverence for the individual soul that we can aid in this consummation. It is not by Chinese policies that China is to be civilized. I believe that the immortal truths of the Declaration of Independence came from the same source with the Golden Rule and the Sermon on the Mount. We can trust Him who promulgated these laws to keep the country safe that obeys them. The laws of the universe have their own sanction. They will not fail.

The power that causes the compass to point to the north, that dismisses the star on its pathway through the skies, promising that in a thousand years it shall return again true to its hour, and keeps His word, will vindicate His own moral law. As surely as the path on which our fathers entered a hundred years ago led to safety, to strength, to glory, so surely will the path on which we now propose to enter bring us to shame, to weakness, and to peril.

7

An Act to Execute Certain Treaty Stipulations Relating to Chinese (Chinese Exclusion Act)[1]

May 6, 1882

After Congress failed to override President Arthur's veto of Senate Bill 71, an act to exclude Chinese immigrants for twenty years, the House moved quickly to consider H.R. 5804, a ten-year exclusion bill, under suspension of the rules, which limited debate to thirty minutes. It passed the House without any trouble, 201 to 37 (53 not voting). The Senate, however, debated the bill for five days, with Democrats reiterating their objections to Chinese immigration and insisting that the bill retain the House definition of "Chinese laborers" as both skilled and unskilled laborers. It passed the Senate, 32 to 15 (29 not voting), reflecting a split among Republicans—9 in favor and 15 opposed. President Arthur approved the bill on May 6, 1882.

Whereas, In the opinion of the Government of the United States the coming of Chinese laborers to this country endangers the good order of certain localities within the territory thereof: Therefore,

Be it enacted by the Senate and House of Representatives of the United States of America in Congress assembled, That from and after the expiration of ninety days next after the passage of this act, and until the

[1]The act was intended to implement the Angell Treaty of 1881, which amended the Burlingame Treaty of 1868. Its popular name, Chinese Exclusion Act, first appeared in the text of the Magnuson Act of 1943, which repealed the exclusion laws and granted Chinese residents naturalization rights.

Chinese Exclusion Act, Pub. L. No. 47–126, 22 Stat. 58 (1882).

expiration of ten years next after the passage of this act, the coming of Chinese laborers to the United States be, and the same is hereby, suspended; and during such suspension it shall not be lawful for any Chinese laborer to come, or, having so come after the expiration of said ninety days, to remain within the United States.

SEC. 2. That the master of any vessel who shall knowingly bring within the United States on such vessel, and land or permit to be landed, any Chinese laborer, from any foreign port or place, shall be deemed guilty of a misdemeanor, and on conviction thereof shall be punished by a fine of not more than five hundred dollars for each and every such Chinese laborer so brought, and may be also imprisoned for a term not exceeding one year.

SEC. 3. That the two foregoing sections shall not apply to Chinese laborers who were in the United States on the seventeenth day of November, eighteen hundred and eighty, or who shall have come into the same before the expiration of ninety days next after the passage of this act, and who shall produce to such master before going on board such vessel, and shall produce to the Collector of the port in the United States at which such vessel shall arrive, the evidence hereinafter in this act required of his being one of the laborers in this section mentioned; nor shall the two foregoing sections apply to the case of any master whose vessel, being bound to a port not within the United States, shall come within the jurisdiction of the United States by reason of being in distress or in stress of weather, or touching at any port of the United States on its voyage to any foreign port or place: *Provided*, That all Chinese laborers brought on such vessel shall depart with the vessel on leaving port.

SEC. 4. That for the purpose of properly identifying Chinese laborers who were in the United States on the seventeenth day of November, eighteen hundred and eighty, or who shall have come into the same before the expiration of ninety days next after the passage of this act, and in order to furnish them with the proper evidence of their right to go from and come to the United States of their free will and accord, as provided by the treaty between the United States and China dated November seventeenth, eighteen hundred and eighty, the collector of customs of the district from which any such Chinese laborer shall depart from the United States shall, in person or by deputy, go on board each vessel having on board any such Chinese laborer and cleared or about to sail from his district for a foreign port, and on such vessel make a list of all such Chinese laborers, which shall be entered in registry-books to be kept for that purpose, in which shall be stated the name, age, occupation, last place of residence, physical marks or peculiarities, and all facts necessary for the identification of each of such Chinese laborers, which books shall be safely kept in the custom-house; and every such Chinese laborer so departing from the United States shall be entitled to, and shall receive free of any charge or cost upon application therefor, from the collector or his deputy, at the time such list is taken, a certificate, signed by the collector or his deputy and attested by his seal of office, in such form as the Secretary of the Treasury shall prescribe, which certificate shall contain a statement of the name, age, occupation, last place of residence, personal description, and facts of identification of the Chinese laborer to whom the certificate is issued, corresponding with the said list and registry in all particulars. In case any Chinese laborer after having received such certificate shall leave such vessel before her departure he shall deliver his certificate to the master of the vessel, and if such Chinese laborer shall fail to return to such vessel before her departure from port the certificate shall be delivered by the master to the collector of customs for cancellation. The certificate herein provided for shall entitle the Chinese laborer to whom the same is issued to return to and re-enter the United States upon producing and delivering the same to the collector of customs of the district at which such Chinese laborer shall seek to re-enter; and upon delivery of such certificate by such Chinese laborer to the collector of customs at the time of re-entry in the United States, said collector shall cause the same to be filed in the custom-house and duly canceled.

SEC. 5. That any Chinese laborer mentioned in section four of this act being in the United States, and desiring to depart from the United States by land, shall have the right to demand and receive, free of charge or cost, a certificate of identification similar to that provided for in section four of this act to be issued to such Chinese laborers as may desire to leave the United States by water; and it is hereby made the duty of the collector of customs of the district next adjoining the foreign country to which said Chinese laborer desires to go to issue such certificate, free of charge or cost, upon application by such Chinese laborer, and to enter the same upon registry-books to be kept by him for the purpose, as provided for in section four of this act.

SEC. 6. That in order to the faithful execution of articles one and two of the treaty in this act before mentioned, every Chinese person other than a laborer who may be entitled by said treaty and this act to come within the United States, and who shall be about to come to the United States, shall be identified as so entitled by the Chinese Government in each case, such identity to be evidenced by a certificate issued under the authority of said government, which certificate shall be in the English language or (if not in the English language) accompanied by a translation into English, stating such right to come, and which certificate shall state the name, title or official rank, if any, the age, height, and all physical peculiarities, former and present occupation or profession, and place of residence in China of the person to whom the certificate is issued and that such person is entitled, conformably to the treaty in this act mentioned to come within the United States. Such certificate shall be prima-facie evidence of the fact set forth therein, and shall be produced to the collector of customs, or his deputy, of the port in the district in the United States at which the person named therein shall arrive.

SEC. 7. That any person who shall knowingly and falsely alter or substitute any name for the name written in such certificate or forge any such certificate, or knowingly utter any forged or fraudulent certificate, or falsely personate any person named in any such certificate, shall be deemed guilty of a misdemeanor; and upon conviction thereof shall be fined in a sum not exceeding one thousand dollars, and imprisoned in a penitentiary for a term of not more than five years.

SEC. 8. That the master of any vessel arriving in the United States from any foreign port or place shall, at the same time he delivers a manifest of the cargo, and if there be no cargo, then at the time of making a report of the entry of the vessel pursuant to law, in addition to the other matter required to be reported, and before landing, or permitting to land, any Chinese passengers, deliver and report to the collector of customs of the district in which such vessels shall have arrived a separate list of all Chinese passengers taken on board his vessel at any foreign port or place, and all such passengers on board the vessel at that time. Such list shall show the names of such passengers (and if accredited officers of the Chinese Government traveling on the business of that government, or their servants, with a note of such facts), and the names and other particulars, as shown by their respective certificates; and such list shall be sworn to by the master in the manner required by law in relation to the manifest of the cargo. Any willful refusal or neglect of any such master to comply with the provisions of this section shall incur the same penalties and forfeiture as are provided for a refusal or neglect to report and deliver a manifest of the cargo.

SEC. 9. That before any Chinese passengers are landed from any such vessel, the collector, or his deputy, shall proceed to examine such passengers, comparing the certificates with the list and with the passengers; and no passenger shall be allowed to land in the United States from such vessel in violation of law.

SEC.10. That every vessel whose master shall knowingly violate any of the provisions of this act shall be deemed forfeited to the United States, and shall be liable to seizure and condemnation in any district of the United States into which such vessel may enter or in which she may be found.

SEC. 11. That any person who shall knowingly bring into or cause to be brought into the United States by land, or who shall knowingly aid or abet the same, or aid or abet the landing in the United States from any vessel of any Chinese person not lawfully entitled to enter the United States, shall be deemed guilty of a misdemeanor, and shall, on conviction thereof, be fined in a sum not exceeding one thousand dollars, and imprisoned for a term not exceeding one year.

SEC. 12. That no Chinese person shall be permitted to enter the United States by land without producing to the proper officer of customs the certificate in this act required of Chinese persons seeking to land from a vessel. And any Chinese person found unlawfully within the United States shall be caused to be removed therefrom to the country from whence he came, by direction of the President of the United States, and at the cost of the United States, after being brought before some justice, judge, or commissioner of a court of the United States and found to be one not lawfully entitled to be or remain in the United States.

SEC.13. That this act shall not apply to diplomatic and other officers of the Chinese Government traveling upon the business of that government, whose credentials shall be taken as equivalent to the certificate in this act mentioned, and shall exempt them and their body and household servants from the provisions of this act as to other Chinese persons.

SEC. 14. That hereafter no State court or court of the United States shall admit Chinese to citizenship; and all laws in conflict with this act are hereby repealed.[2]

SEC.15. That the words "Chinese laborers", wherever used in this act, shall be construed to mean both skilled and unskilled laborers and Chinese employed in mining.

Approved, May 6, 1882.

---

[2]Although the Naturalization Laws of 1790 and 1870 as well as the Burlingame Treaty of 1868 stopped Chinese from becoming naturalized citizens, certain state courts were granting them citizenship. This law marked the first time that Congress prohibited admission to citizenship by race.

2

Representations of the Chinese in the Popular Press

8

BRET HARTE

The Heathen Chinee

1870

Born in Albany, New York, in 1836, Bret Harte moved to California with his family in 1854, where he pursued mining, teaching, and journalism. Harte had a track record of opposing racial prejudice and hostilities against Native Americans and the Chinese, and he wrote the poem, "Plain Language from Truthful James," for the Overland Monthly *in 1870 to satirize anti-Chinese sentiment among Irish workers in California. The poem became an international sensation and was republished as "The Heathen Chinee" in numerous publications. Years later, Harte called it "the worst poem I ever wrote," because readers had misconstrued the poem to read that Chinese were indeed "cheap labor," "heathens," and "wily tricksters."*

Bret Harte, "Plain Language from Truthful James," *Overland Monthly*, September 1870, 287–88.

PLAIN LANGUAGE FROM TRUTHFUL JAMES
(Table Mountain, 1870)

Which I wish to remark—
    And my language is plain—
That for ways that are dark
    And for tricks that are vain,
The heathen Chinee is peculiar,
    Which the same I would rise to explain.

Ah Sin was his name;
    And I shall not deny
In regard to the same
    What that name might imply,
But his smile it was pensive and child-like,
    As I frequent remarked to Bill Nye.

It was August the third;
    And quite soft was the skies;
Which it might be inferred
    That Ah Sin was likewise;
Yet he played it that day upon William
    And me in a way I despise.

Which we had a small game,
    And Ah Sin took a hand:
It was Euchre. The same
    He did not understand;
But he smiled as he sat by the table,
    With the smile that was child-like and bland.

Yet the cards they were stocked
    In a way that I grieve,
And my feelings were shocked
    At the state of Nye's sleeve:
Which was stuffed full of aces and bowers,
    And the same with intent to deceive.

But the hands that were played
    By that heathen Chinee,

And the points that he made,
　　Were quite frightful to see—
Till at last he put down a right bower,
　　Which the same Nye had dealt unto me.

Then I looked up at Nye,
　　And he gazed upon me;
And he rose with a sigh,
　　And said, "Can this be?
We are ruined by Chinese cheap labor"—
　　And he went for that heathen Chinee.

In the scene that ensued
　　I did not take a hand,
But the floor it was strewed
　　Like the leaves on the strand
With the cards that Ah Sin had been hiding,
　　In the game "he did not understand."

In his sleeves, which were long,
　　He had twenty-four packs—
Which was coming it strong,
　　Yet I state but the facts;
And we found on his nails, which were taper,
　　What is frequent in tapers—that's wax.

Which is why I remark,
　　And my language is plain,
That for ways that are dark,
　　And for tricks that are vain,
The heathen Chinee is peculiar—
　　Which the same I am free to maintain.

Rough on Rats
1880s

Trade cards were widely used in the late nineteenth century to promote products and services. This advertisement for the "Rough on Rats" pesticide capitalizes on and perpetuates false claims that the Chinese were lowering the standard of living, spreading diseases, and eating rats.

Courtesy Lenore-Metrick Chen Collection

Opium Den
1877

In the wake of the Chinese Exclusion Act, San Francisco Chinatown became a favorite attraction for wealthy white Americans "slumming" as urban tourists. Newspapers played up on the deep fascination with the supposed Chinese propensity for vice, especially opium smoking, as well as sensational moral panics that white women were becoming addicts in Chinese opium dens. These images of Chinese moral degeneracy helped reinforce Chinese exclusion, but they also sustained the American attraction to Chinatowns as exotic enclaves within modern urban environments.

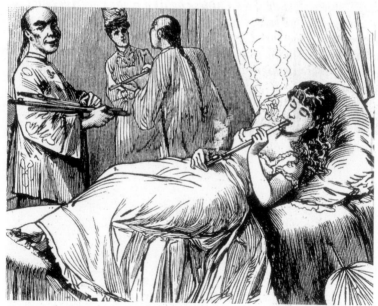

11

THOMAS NAST

The Chinese Question

1871

American caricaturist Thomas Nast was born in Landau, Germany, in 1840. When he was six, his family immigrated to New York City, where he attended school until he was fourteen. Nast started working as a draftsman for Frank Leslie's Illustrated Newspaper *in 1856 and was associated with* Harper's Weekly *magazine from 1862 to 1886. Many of his political cartoons reflect his anti-Catholic and anti-Irish sentiments as well as his support for Native Americans and Chinese immigrants. In "The Chinese Question," Nast draws Columbia, symbolizing America and its cardinal rule of "equality for all," shielding a dejected Chinese against a gang of Irish thugs. The imagery in the back alludes to the Civil War draft riots, when Irish mobs in New York City burned the Colored Orphan Asylum and lynched blacks. On the wall behind Columbia are plastered racist slurs against Chinese immigrants often espoused by proponents of Chinese exclusion.*

Thomas Nast, "The Chinese Question," *Harper's Weekly*, February 18, 1871, 149.

Courtesy of the Philip P. Choy Collection

12

GEORGE FREDERICK KELLER

"What Shall We Do with Our Boys?"

1882

Born in Prussia, George Frederick Keller arrived in San Francisco in the late 1860s. A talented cigar box lithographer and part-time cartoonist, he was hired by The Wasp *to draw fear-mongering images that depict the Chinese as ruthless competitors in the labor market. In the following political cartoon, Keller draws the Chinese as an eleven-handed monster who deprives wholesome American boys (right frame) of honest jobs in certain trades and crafts that he dominated. The satchel of money (top left corner) indicates that the Chinese do not invest in America but send their savings home to families in China. Keller imbues the Chinese worker with a gleeful, sinister expression as his queue rises in mid-air, propelled by the frenzy of his windmill-like hands.*

George Frederick Keller, "What Shall We Do with Our Boys?" *The Wasp*, March 3, 1882, 136–37.

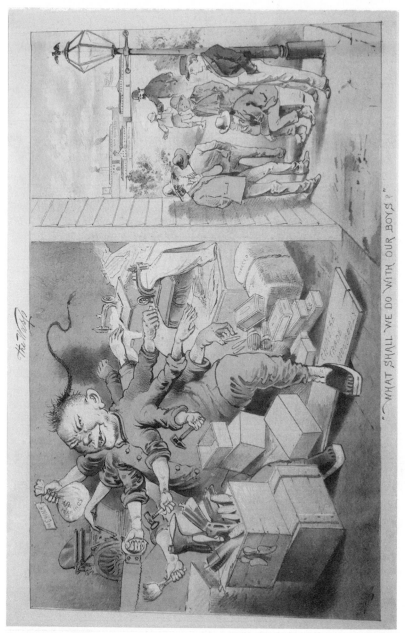

Courtesy of the Philip P. Choy Collection.

13

GEORGE FREDERICK KELLER

A Statue for Our Harbor

1881

The Statue of Liberty in New York was still under construction when this political cartoon appeared in The Wasp. *Featuring a Chinese man in tattered clothes, rat tail-like queue, and stereotypical facial features, holding an opium pipe with his foot resting on a skull, California's imitation of the Statue of Liberty was intended to show readers how Chinese immigrants, laden with "Filth, Immorality, Diseases, and Ruin to White Labor," will overrun the West and destroy the nation itself.*

George Frederick Keller, "A Statue for Our Harbor," *The Wasp*, November 11, 1881, 320.

A STATUE FOR *OUR* HARBOR.

Courtesy of the Philip P. Choy Collection.

14

JAMES ALBERT WALES

"Where Both Platforms Agree"

1880

Born in Clyde, Ohio, in 1852, James Albert Wales studied art in London and Paris. He became the chief cartoonist for Leslie's Illustrated Newspaper *before going to work for* Puck, *the nation's premiere journal of graphic humor and political satire. Wales left* Puck *in 1881 to found* Judge, *a competitor color weekly. By the time of the 1880 election, both political parties had adopted anti-Chinese platforms. Wales captured this view best in a cover illustrating presidential candidates James Garfield (left) and Winfield Scott Hancock (right) nailing a Chinese immigrant between two "anti-Chinese" boards labeled "Republican Plank" and "Democratic Plank." Without naturalization rights and the vote, the Chinese were of no use to either party.*

James Albert Wales, "Where Both Platforms Agree—No Vote—No Use to Either Party," *Puck*, July 14, 1880.

Courtesy of the Philip P. Choy Collection.

15

FRIEDRICH GRAETZ

The Anti-Chinese Wall

1882

Friedrich Graetz, an Austrian-born satirical artist, came to the United States in 1882 to work for Puck. *He spoke little English and needed precise instructions in drawing American political cartoons. "The Anti-Chinese Wall" shows Uncle Sam using "Congressional Mortar" and building blocks carried by American workers of different ethnicities to build a wall against Chinese immigration. Meanwhile, Chinese workers across the ocean are shown dismantling the Great Wall to permit American traders and missionaries to enter China—an indication that China, but not America, was abiding by the reciprocity clause of the Burlingame Treaty. In an age of partisan politics, the weekly magazine played an important role as a nonpartisan crusader for good government and American constitutional ideals.*

Friedrich Graetz, "The Anti-Chinese Wall," *Puck*, March 29, 1882, 56–57.

Courtesy of the Philip P. Choy Collection.

3

Enforcing the Chinese Exclusion Laws

16

JOHN H. WISE

Letters Sent by the Collector

1895

Born in Accomack County, Virginia, John H. Wise moved to San Francisco in 1853 to begin work in the Custom House. A staunch Democrat, he was elected to the San Francisco Board of Supervisors in 1875 and appointed Collector of Customs by President Glover Cleveland in 1892. He served in that capacity until 1898. A strict enforcer of the Chinese exclusion laws, Wise made up his own rules, such as requiring "convincing proof" of the exempt status and marriages of Chinese merchants as well as the testimony of two white witnesses to support the claims of U.S. citizenship. He prohibited Chinese detainees from speaking to their attorneys and often denied them entry based on minor discrepancies in their cross-examinations. Wise had a running battle with the district courts, which reversed over half of his decisions upon appeal for being unreasonable and lacking in good faith. Yet, as the following letters show, he took pride in being a "tough" but "just" gatekeeper against Chinese fraudulent entries.

Copies of Non-Departmental Letters Sent by the Collector and the Deputy Collector, June 11, 1861–1914. RG 36, Records of U.S. Customs Service, Collection District of San Francisco, CA. National Archives, San Francisco; Copies of Letters Sent by the Collector to the Secretary of the Treasury, June 1, 1861–October 5, 1912. RG 36, Records of U.S. Customs Service, Collection District of San Francisco, CA. National Archives, San Francisco.

Feb. 26, 1895.

W. F. Thompson
Fresno, Cal.
Sir:—

I respectfully acknowledge the receipt of your letter of 20th instant, inquiring if a Chinese merchant now residing in this country, is entitled to bring his wife and minor children into the United States and if so what proofs must be made.

In reply you are advised that under the ruling of the Treasury Department the wife and children of tender years, of a merchant legally domiciled in the U.S., have a right to land on arrival on proof satisfactory to the Collector at the port of arrival, that she is his wife according to our understanding of the marriage relation, and that the children were born in wedlock. In view of the wide door to fraud opened by such ruling, and of the great difficulty in obtaining adequate proof of the marriage of Chinese and birth of their children, I have deemed it incumbent on me to be very cautious. I cannot say what proof I would accept, certainly not the unsupported testimony of the Chinese themselves. If they had a certificate from the U.S. Consul at the port of departure that he had investigated the case and was satisfied the woman is the wife and the children those of the Chinese merchant now in this country, it would be of some import, but I would not bind myself to accept it absolutely. In fact I shall do as much as I can to discourage Chinese in this country from sending for their alleged wives and children, because I am satisfied that great frauds would be perpetuated and many women and young girls brought for immoral purposes under the guise of wives and children, and it is a well known fact that the cunning of Chinese often circumvent the vigilance of the Customs officers.

Respectfully yours,
John H. Wise
Collector

* * *

October 15, 1895.

Secretary of the Treasury
Washington, D.C.
Sir:

I beg to submit for the consideration of the Department the following statements of facts:

Jong Pong, a Chinese laborer, who is known by the American name of Sam Smith, arrived at this port in July last and brought his two sons, who established the fact that they were born in the United States, and they were landed. Jong Pong came to California in 1849, but went to China as a laborer before the recent treaty was adopted, and, although he was a registered laborer, he could not obtain a return certificate at the time of his departure and therefore could not legally land in the United States. At the request of Mr. Lloyd Tevis[1] I landed him temporarily as in transit and he is now about to depart for China on the steamer which sails on the 22nd instant. He desires, however, to return to the United States and remain here; also to bring his wife, Ah Choy, and his daughter, Ah Ying. The daughter is a "small-footed" woman[2] and was born in the United States. She comes back to the United States to be married, and, having been born in the United States, can be landed.

Jong Pong is 67 years old, speaks English well, and has adopted American clothes, and has considerable property. He wishes to return to China on the steamer which sails on the 22nd instant, to bring his wife and daughter. If, under the circumstances, the Department decides that he may now be landed, a certificate can be issued to him, entitling him to return. The question would then be in regard to his wife. Under the ruling of the Courts the wife takes the status of the husband, and they have also ruled that the wife of a laborer, who is domiciled in the United States, cannot be landed but inasmuch as the wife of Jong Pong was previously in the United States, as a matter of equity in this particular case, if her husband could be given a return certificate, it would seem that she should be landed. Jong Pong says, if his wife cannot be landed, he will stay in China, but having lived in the United States so long, he desires to end his days here. He is vouched for as a man of strict integrity by very responsible persons.

His case is submitted for such action as the Department may deem proper, and if you should decide that he may now be landed and a certificate issued for his return, and that his wife can also be landed, please wire your decision, collect, in order that he may be advised by the time the steamer sails.

Respectfully yours,
John H. Wise
Collector.

[1] A banker and capitalist, Lloyd Tevis was president of Wells Fargo Bank from 1872 to 1892.
[2] Bound feet were considered a mark of wealth and gentility in China and a sign to immigrant inspectors that a woman was not a prostitute.

17

TERENCE V. POWDERLY

Exclude Anarchist and Chinaman!

1901

Born in Carbondale, Pennsylvania, to Irish Catholic immigrants, Terence V. Powderly served as mayor of Scranton (1878–1884), head of the Knights of Labor union (1879–1893), and commissioner-general of immigration (1897–1902). During his administration, Powderly set new policies that called for narrower definitions of the exempt classes, tighter border control, arbitrary raids and arrests, and the extension of the Chinese exclusion laws to Hawaii and the Philippines. He hired inspectors of like mind who were pro-labor and anti-Chinese, instructing them to "exclude when in doubt." The following two articles by Powderly, written and published in prominent periodicals while he was commissioner-general of immigration, showcase his strong ties to organized labor and his racist views toward Chinese immigration. Originally appointed by President William McKinley to the position of commissioner-general as a reward for his campaign work in the 1896 presidential election, Powderly was dismissed from the position by President Theodore Roosevelt in 1902 for his mishandling of reforms at Ellis Island. He was, however, reinstated as chief of the Immigration Bureau's Division of Information from 1907 to 1921.

AN APPALLING MENACE TO AMERICAN LABOR

The opposition to the Chinese coolie is not alone because of his race or his religion, but because of the economic position he occupies in this country. No graver danger has ever menaced the workingmen of America than that which faces them when the possibility of lowering

T. V. Powderly, Commissioner-General of Immigration, "Exclude Anarchist and Chinaman!," *Collier's Weekly*, December 14, 1901, 5, 7; T. V. Powderly, "A Bouquet of New Year Wishes by Distinguished Men," *Washington Times*, January 1, 1902, 8.

the bars at our seaports and border-lines to the Chinese is presented. They do not assimilate with our people, do not wear our clothing, do not adopt our customs, language, religion, or sentiments. It is said that the Chinese, if given an opportunity, will become Americanized. The Chinese coolie will no more become Americanized than an American can take on the habit, customs, garb and religion of the Mongolian. Chinese have lived in San Francisco for over fifty years, and, with the exception of an increased population, Chinatown is now as it was in the beginning. American and Chinese civilizations are antagonistic; they cannot live and thrive and both survive on the same soil. One or the other must perish.

Much can be said on the question, and to deal with it properly, fairly and impartially more space should be devoted to the treatment of the subject than can be given here.

It will be said that such details as are here suggested would, if required by law, prove expensive, and that a great deal of labor would be required to maintain such a system of treating aliens. I grant that it would cost more than the present system, but this is not a cheap country, and if it is worth living in, it is worth defending at any cost.

Such a plan would not be so expensive as the uninitiated might suppose. We already have the machinery in operation, but few additional inspectors would be required, and, with a corps of efficient officials operating inland and abroad, the work could be promptly and properly done. Space cannot here be given to the details of this proposed innovation, but that it can easily be set in motion and as easily continued is beyond question.

WELCOME TO ACCEPTABLE IMMIGRANTS

T.V. Powderly, Commissioner General of Immigration—It is my wish that during the new year only such foreigners will come to this country as will make good citizens. To these we always extend our welcome, but the others we must exclude for our own good. I wish that the day when there came here those sturdy men of Scotland, Germany, Ireland, and Scandinavia, who built up the great Northwest and other regions of this country, would return, and that whatever is done, the Chinese will be kept out.

18

NG POON CHEW

The Treatment of the Exempt Classes of Chinese in the United States

1908

The harsh and humiliating treatment of the Chinese exempt classes by immigration officers at the U.S. borders ultimately led to the 1905 boycott of American goods in China. Among the ardent supporters of the boycott in America was Ng Poon Chew, editor of the Chung Sai Yat Po *(Chinese American daily), a progressive newspaper that favored reform in China and advocated equal rights for Chinese in America. A native of Guangdong Province, Ng immigrated to the United States in 1881 with high hopes of making his fortune. Instead, he converted to Christianity while studying English at a Presbyterian mission in San Jose, California, going on to graduate from the San Francisco Theological Seminary and become an ordained minister in 1892. A popular speaker on the Chautauqua and Lyceum circuits, Ng Poon Chew was one of the few educated Chinese Americans capable of speaking out against anti-Chinese legislation and discriminatory practices. When he was sent by the Chinese Six Companies on a national speaking tour to defend the Chinese position, he had published the following pamphlet to critique the unfair treatment of the exempt classes.*

After a quarter of a century of Chinese Exclusion, many people take it for granted that Exclusion has become a fixed policy of the Government of the United States, and that the vexed Chinese question is finally and permanently settled, as far as the country is concerned. The exclusion of Chinese laborers may have become a fixed policy with the United States, but the treatment of the exempt classes is not settled and will not be until it is settled aright with justice to all.

Ng Poon Chew, *The Treatment of the Exempt Classes of Chinese in the United States: A Statement from the Chinese in America* (San Francisco: *Chung Sai Yat Po*, 1908).

The Chinese Exclusion Law, as now enacted and enforced, is in violation of the letter and spirit of the treaty between this country and China, and also in opposition to the original intention of Congress on the subject. As long as this law remains on the statute books in its present shape, and is carried out by methods such as are now in vogue, the Chinese question will continue to be a vexatious one in the United States, as well as a fruitful source of irritation between America and China; and it will continue to hinder the upbuilding of commercial interests between the two great countries.

During twenty-five years the Chinese exclusion policy has steadily increased in stringency; as Senator Hoar said on the floor of Congress, the United States enforced the exclusion laws first with water, then with vinegar, and then with red pepper, and at last with vitriol. The Exclusion Law has been carried out with such vigor that it has almost become an extermination law. The Chinese population in the United States has been reduced from 150,000 in 1880 to 65,000 at the present time. During those twenty-five years much injustice and wrong have been heaped upon the Chinese people by the United States in the execution of the exclusion policy, and now it is time that this great nation should calmly review the whole question thoroughly and revise the law, so that it may come within the spirit of the treaty, and at the same time fulfill the original intention of Congress, namely: the exclusion of Chinese laborers, and the admission of all other classes. . . .

The unwarranted limitation of the exempt classes of the Chinese — who have a right to come under both treaties and laws — to a few persons of a very few occupations, has come about chiefly through political agitation to secure the votes of workingmen, and by the strong anti-Chinese prejudice of immigration officers, who were themselves often representatives of labor organizations. All Chinese, except laborers, had a right to come and go freely under the treaty and even under the first restriction law of 1882, and this was acknowledged by both nations for eighteen years, although immigration officials, in some instances, enlarged the definition of laborers so as to include persons not technically of that class.

But in 1898 the Attorney General of the United States decided that the true theory of the law was not that all Chinese who were not laborers could come in, but that only those could come who were expressly named in the law. If this were correct, the law itself was a violation of the treaty; but, in fact this ruling violated the clear and originally accepted meaning of the treaty and of the laws passed in execution of it. The American immigration officials, however, made it a pretext for excluding all the Chinese they could, even of the five classes named in the treaty. It appeared to be their ambition to deny all Chinese admission, and any one admitted was regarded as a lost case. The phrase "officials, teachers, students, merchants and travelers for curiosity or pleasure," was used in the treaty merely by way of illustration and before 1898 had been generally so interpreted, but the Attorney General's decision gave opportunity for limiting even these classes still further.[1]

From this time on the exempt classes of Chinese were limited by enlarging the definition of laborers to include many who were not laborers, and by narrowing the definitions of teacher, student and merchant so as to exclude many who were certainly of these classes. For instance, it was declared that a teacher was one who teaches the higher branches in a recognized institution of learning; a student was one who pursues the higher branches in a recognized institution of learning, facilities for which are wanting in his own country or in the country from which he came; a merchant was one who carried on business in a fixed place, in buying and selling, in his own name. If a merchant, who does a million dollars' worth of business a year, invests one dollar in a hotel or restaurant business or in a manufacturing concern, in a mining venture or railroad enterprise, his status as a merchant is at once vitiated, and he is denied admission, or deported if already admitted. As a result Chinese traders, salesmen, clerks, buyers, bookkeepers, bankers, accountants, managers, storekeepers, agents, cashiers, interpreters, physicians, proprietors of restaurants and laundries, employers, actors, newspaper editors, and even preachers and missionaries of Christianity, are excluded from the shores of the United States. A Chinese boy by the name of Wah Sang was admitted to this country as a student in theology, and as long as he was a student he was allowed to remain in the country; but when he completed his course in theological training, and entered into active service in preaching the Gospel to his countrymen under the auspices of the Methodist Church, he was arrested in Texas as a laborer, was tried and ordered deported in February, 1905, the court sustaining the contention of the immigration officials that a preacher is a laborer, and therefore subject to the operation of the Exclusion Law.

The exclusion by regulation, not justified by treaties or laws, has been carried much further so as to harass and inconvenience Chinese merchants, students and others in many ways. The United States demands a certificate of admission with many personal details, signed by officials of the Chinese Government and the United States; but when the certificate

---

[1] 22 Op. Attorney General 132 (1898). See Salyer, *Laws Harsh as Tigers*, 65.

has been secured in proper form and every requirement has been met, the holder is not sure of being able to enter the United States; for the immigration officials re-examine him and often detain and sometimes deport him on petty technicalities. For the practice with the immigration officials is to regard every Chinese applicant for admission as a cheat, a liar, a rogue and a criminal, and they proceed to examine him with the aim in mind of seeing how he may be excluded, rather than of finding out whether he is legally entitled to land. For many years the certificate has been no guarantee that its holder could be admitted, though he might be a great merchant or a student coming to study at an American university. . . .

Furthermore, Chinese residents of the exempt class are limited and harassed by official regulations in going to and from China, in bringing in their wives and children, and in many ways are treated as the subjects of other nations are never treated by the United States. Ladies of highly respectable families have been asked all sorts of questions in the examinations by the immigration officials which they would not dare to mention in the hearing of American ladies. A boy of ten years of age, whose father was a prominent merchant, arrived in San Francisco with his parents. After a long investigation the parents were admitted and the boy ordered deported on the ground that he had *trachoma*, although the American officers at the port of departure had given them a health certificate, and although Americans on board the vessel testified that the ship's doctor had examined the eyes of all the second cabin passengers without disinfecting his hands. The Secretary of Commerce and Labor refused to reverse the decision of deportation. There have been a number of instances where Chinese merchants returning from a trip to China with their wives and families have been allowed to land but have had their wives and children deported. . . .

For years the *Bertillon System*, used for the identification of criminals in the United States, has also been used to identify departing Chinese of all classes who wished to return.[2] The system has only been abandoned during the last few months because the Department at Washington failed to supply the different Bureaus with sufficient men to operate it.

---

[2]Invented by a French criminologist and used on Chinese immigrants, the Bertillon System involved taking detailed measurements of the naked body to distinguish one Chinese applicant from another and to detect fraudulent entries. Ng Poon Chew regarded the system of minute measurements "a great humiliation." See Lee, *At America's Gates*, 84–85.

Although the Geary Law of 1893 [1892], which required resident Chinese laborers to obtain a certificate of residence and to be photographed, did not require the exempt classes nor their wives and children to obtain a certificate, the regulations of the immigration bureau require officials to arrest every Chinese found without a certificate. Consequently any Chinese merchant, student or physician who was in the country at the time of registration and did not get a certificate is now liable to arrest and imprisonment.

Under these regulations many of the exempt classes have been held up in various ways, at many places and times, by the immigration officials in their zeal to enforce the Chinese Exclusion Laws. The exempt classes, thus arrested, are put to great expense and inconveniences before they are released by United States Commissioners. Once an attaché of the Chinese Legation at Washington was held up while traveling through Arizona on official business, and put to much inconvenience and indignity before he was released by order of the Department at Washington. In order to find some who might be without certificates, the whole Chinese quarter in Denver and in Boston was surrounded, and all Chinese found without certificates, whether merchants or no, were arrested and herded in close confinement, until their status was decided by the court. . . .

It is well known that the discourteous treatment of merchants and students by immigration officials was the principal cause of the boycott of American products in China in 1905. Although this boycott was shortly suppressed by the Chinese Government, it was an expression of the bad feeling which had arisen between the two countries because of violation of the treaty and accumulated sense of injustice. Thirty years ago there were nearly 200 Chinese students in the United States pursuing their education; when they returned to China they became leaders of the people and reported that the Americans were a friendly and honorable nation. But since the passage of the Geary Law especially, students of all grades except post-graduate have been excluded. They go to other countries, and when they return to China do not speak favorably of the United States; and those who have received indignities in America have also returned home full of resentment, and urge their countrymen to resist the violation of the treaty.

The ill-treatment of those who were entitled to come in as freely as other nationalities has been unhappy not only in producing irritation and unfriendly feeling where formerly there was friendly feeling, but it has been disastrous also to commercial interests. Because of injustice all the great Chinese merchants who formerly paid one-third of the customs duties at the port of San Francisco, have gone back to China or do business in other countries. Although there are now few merchants of first rank in San Francisco, the Chinese importers still pay a large proportion of the customs duties. If all classes of merchants, traders and business men had been encouraged to come and go freely it is probable that the trade between China and America would have increased rapidly and would now be much greater than it is. At the present time American exports to China are decreasing; the volume of exports to China during the year 1907 decreased fifty per cent from that of the year 1906.

Chinese laborers of all classes have been excluded from the United States by mutual agreement, and the Chinese themselves are not now asking for any change in this arrangement; but they do ask for as fair treatment as other nationalities receive in relation to the exempt classes. Since the first restriction law was passed the United States has received as immigrants more than two million Austro-Hungarians, two million Italians and a million and a half Russians and Finns. Each of these totals is from five to seven times the whole amount of Chinese immigration of all classes during thirty years of free immigration, seventy times the amount of immigration of the Chinese who were not laborers. Even if the number of the exempts under a just interpretation of the treaty should rise to 10,000 in one year, it would still be less than one-hundredth of the total immigration to the United States in one year. During the fiscal year 1907 there came to the United States from Europe 1,280,000 immigrants; whereas, during the thirty years of free Chinese immigration, the largest number of Chinese found at any one time in the United States was one hundred and fifty thousand.

The question is not now of the admission of laborers, but whether other Chinese who are entitled to come under both law and treaty shall receive the same courtesies as people of other nations, and shall be relieved from many harassing regulations. They must no longer be detained, photographed and examined as if they were suspected of crime. Americans desire to build up a large trade with the Orient, but they can scarcely expect to succeed if the United States Government continues to sanction the illegal and unfriendly treatment of Chinese subjects. President Roosevelt has said that if the United States expects justice it must do justice to the Chinese, and certainly the Americans cannot expect to obtain the trade of the Orient by treating the Chinese with discourtesy.

19

OSCAR S. STRAUS

Chinese Immigration

1907

In 1906, President Theodore Roosevelt appointed Oscar Straus—a Jewish immigrant, lawyer, businessman, and former ambassador to the Ottoman Empire, to the cabinet post of secretary of commerce and labor. In this position, Straus oversaw the operations of the Immigration Bureau. As the following annual report demonstrates, Straus shared Roosevelt's view that the Chinese exclusion laws should be enforced on a class rather than race basis—all Chinese except laborers should be admitted. Wanting to regain the goodwill of China and uphold American principles of justice and equality, Straus replaced many of T. V. Powderly's restrictive policies with new regulations that liberalized the definition of students and merchants, facilitated the travels of exempt classes in transit, abandoned the Bertillon system, and stopped arbitrary immigration raids in the Chinese communities. He left his cabinet post in 1909 at the end of Roosevelt's term of office but remained in public service, first as U.S. ambassador to Turkey and later as chairman of the New York Public Service Commission.

The present policy of the United States with reference to Chinese immigration, as developed by both the legislative and the executive departments of the Government, is of long standing, having existed for nearly a generation. A governmental policy as long pursued is not lightly to be changed, nor is any change proposed. What I have to urge is not only based upon a full recognition of the fixed character of the present policy, but is entirely in furtherance thereof. It is not the policy of the Government with reference to Chinese immigration that I would criticize, but the manner in which it is of necessity carried out, by reason of the way in which the laws are framed. It had never been the purpose of the Government, as would appear from its laws

---

Annual Report of the Secretary of Commerce and Labor, 1907 (Washington, DC: Government Printing Office, 1907), 15–19.

and treaties, to exclude persons of the Chinese race merely because they are Chinese, regardless of the class to which they belong, and without reference to their age, sex, culture or occupation, or to the object of their coming or their length of stay. The real purpose of the Government's policy is to exclude a particular and well-defined class, leaving other classes of Chinese, except as they, together with all other foreigners, may be included within the prohibitions of the general immigration laws, as free to come and go as the citizens of any other nation. As the laws are framed, however, it would appear that the purpose was rigidly to exclude persons of the Chinese race in general, and to admit only such persons of the race as fall within certain expressly stated exemptions — as if, in other words, exclusion was the rule and admission the exception. I regard this feature of the present laws as unnecessary and fraught with irritating consequences. In the administration of laws so framed, notwithstanding the care taken to treat persons of the Chinese race lawfully entitled to admission with the same courtesy and consideration shown to other foreigners, it is impossible that persons who have to endure requirements and formalities peculiar to themselves should fail to take offense, and to resent as a humiliation the manner in which by law they are distinguished from natives of other countries. Laws so framed can only be regarded as involving a discrimination on account of race, color, previous condition, or religion are alike opposed to the principles of the Republic and to the spirit of the institutions.

It is not surprising, therefore, that both the Chinese Government and the Chinese people should feel aggrieved, and should in various ways manifest their resentment and displeasure. The attitude of the Chinese Government may be inferred from the fact that, in 1904, after the convention of 1894 had been in force for ten years, China, availing herself of a right reserved, formally denounced the treaty, thus refusing longer to be a party to an arrangement which, as carried into effect by legislation was offensive to her national pride. It is not improbable that one of the reasons which led to this action on the part of the Chinese Government was the interpretation which came to be placed upon the treaty and laws relating to Chinese immigration. The understanding in China, her officials contended, was that the object both of the treaty and the laws was to keep out laborers, and that it was never intended that the enumeration of certain exempt classes should operate as an exclusion of all other classes and of laborers besides. This interpretation was rejected, and the necessary effect of all the laws on the subject was declared to be that not only those Chinese should be excluded who are particularly and expressly forbidden entrance, namely, Chinese laborers, but that only those may be admitted who are expressly allowed, although it was admitted that there was authority for the opposite view, and that the Supreme Court had never decided the matter (see correspondence between the Chinese minister and the Secretary of State, 4 Moore's Int. L. Dig., 217). For proof of the feeling of the Chinese people it is only necessary to refer to the boycott of American goods, inaugurated by various trade guilds and business and commercial associations of the Empire during the summer of 1905. While this boycott was happily of short duration and its immediate effects were not as serious as they might have been, the importance of the boycott, as an indication of the degree to which American commercial interests in China are menaced, is not to be overlooked. . . .

But on higher grounds than those of mere commercial self-interest should the frame of the laws be changed. The relations between China and the United States have always been most friendly. It is not only the right but the duty of this Government, for its own protection and for the security and welfare of its citizens, to exclude foreigners from its territory whenever the public interests require, but to so exercise that right as needlessly to offend the amour propre of a friendly nation, or unnecessarily to humiliate a whole people when only a particular class is to be reached, can not be the action intended, and should be guarded against in every possible way. A change in the established policy of rigidly excluding Chinese laborers of every description, both skilled and unskilled, is not even suggested. This policy has been and will continue to be as effectively enforced as circumstances will permit. At a time when the policy of exclusion has been so thoroughly applied that there remain in the United States only about 70,000 Chinese, or less than one-tenth of 1 per cent of the total population, little danger need be apprehended from a full and fair consideration of the whole subject and a recasting of the laws upon a juster basis. During the past fiscal year only 857 Chinese persons were newly admitted to the United States; of the balance of those admitted, all of whom were prior residents, 855 were native-born citizens, 733 were merchants, and only 765 were laborers. As against the total admissions, moreover, there were 336 deportations and an unknown number of voluntary departures. In view of this showing, a more opportune moment than the present can hardly be desired for reaching a better understanding with China on the subject of Chinese immigration and for adjusting our policy in this regard to the demands of justice and equality. This could be done, not by making it any easier for Chinese laborers to enter, but by so framing our laws and treaties as to make admission the rule and exclusion the exception. . . .

During the past year I have been able by departmental regulation to take several steps with a view to the better administration of the Chinese immigration laws. Among others the following may be mentioned:

Owing to the relatively small number of persons in the United States who are familiar with the various dialects, and the still smaller number who are able to read and write the language and to correctly render it into English, and vice versa, the Department has in the past experienced considerable difficulty in securing reliable and competent Chinese interpreters. Rumors having reached the Department to the effect that some of the Chinese interpreters were incompetent, coupled with intimations, unsupported by proof, that others were in collusion with those interested in the unlawful landing of Chinese, in order to test the efficiency of the service and to break up improper associations, if any, growing out of long continued service at one port, I ordered the transfer of practically every Chinese interpreter to a new station, and have besides designated two interpreters of proved ability and honesty to visit each port which such persons are employed for the purpose of conducting a rigid examination as to their competency as well as their honesty. This arrangement, I am confident, will be productive of good results.

It has come to the attention of the Department that domiciled Chinese laborers who are desirous of visiting their native country have considered themselves bound to employ the services of attorneys and others to fill out their applications for return certificates, thereby incurring a charge ranging from $5 to $25 in each case, and possibly a larger fee. Believing such an expense to be entirely unnecessary and that such a practice readily leads to extortion, instructions have been issued to officers of the Chinese immigration service at the various ports to inform all Chinese of this class that all applications for return certificates will be drawn by immigration officers without charge.

20

JOHN D. NAGLE

Exposing the Ramifications of the Coaching Evil

January 15, 1925

A native San Franciscan and Republican, John D. Nagle served in the district attorney and sheriff's offices before assuming his post as commissioner of immigration at Angel Island from 1923 to 1933. By then, the strategies adopted by Chinese immigrants to circumvent the Chinese exclusion laws were proving successful. Between 1910 and 1924, an average of 93 percent of Chinese applicants were admitted into the country, many by falsely claiming to be the sons or daughters of merchants or native-born citizens. Commissioner Nagle made a career of outwitting the "clever" Chinese at their game, spending several years collecting statistical data on the skewed sex ratio of Chinese applicants as proof of their false claims. Lacking reliable documentary evidence to verify Chinese births and family relationships, gatekeepers like Nagle could only hope to expose and entrap fraudulent entries via intensive cross-examinations and by putting a stop to the "coaching evil."

U. S. DEPARTMENT OF LABOR
IMMIGRATION SERVICE

In answering refer to

No. 12016/2934

Office of the Commissioner

Angel Island Station

Via Ferry Post Office

San Francisco, Calif.

Jan. 15, 1925

File 55452, Subject Correspondence, 1906–32, Records of the Immigration and Naturalization Service, RG 85, National Archives, Washington, DC.

Hon. W. W. Husband,

Commissioner-General of Immigration,

Washington, D. C.

Herewith you will find what we apprehend to be the most imposing series of documents ever coming into the hands of this Immigration Service, elucidating the methods employed to secure the admission of Chinese and exposing the ramifications of the coaching evil, which has practically reached perfection under the present system of affairs.

These documents make a voluminous file, this not-withstanding, we very urgently request that the Bureau and Department scrutinize each one of them, as only by doing so will the seriousness of the situation become evident.

Yip Sing, the "Steerer" in this instance, is no different than numerous others engaged in similar practices, among them Who Tong and Jew Shep, whose activities are known to the Bureau and Department. Yip Sing is connected with the Nanking Fook Wo Co., San Francisco, one of the largest mercantile establishments in Chinatown. His specialty, assisted by his brother Yip Nging, is handling cases involving U.S. citizenship. We have consulted his record and we observe that his coaching paper is dated May 17, 1910 and his examination by this service for Form 430 was held May 27, 1910. The points touched upon during the examination accord very materially with those contained in the coaching paper, suggesting possible collusion.

His records of other cases are such as to make him master of the situations involving discrepancies in testimony before the Immigration authorities when any of his many cases are concerned. There are coaching papers and books prepared for use before applicants left China and there are coaching letters that reached him from applicants while in our detention sheds. There are maps of villages covered in details of the minutest character. One of the coaching books is in printed form to permit of inserting appropriate answers to the printed questions. There is a triplicate typewritten copy of one of our own immigration records. There are photographs of applicants, witnesses, prospective applicants and copies of photographs in immigration records. There are copies of important points appearing in records, such as records of trips, family histories, etc., presumably obtained from records that were used as exhibits in excluded cases which made them available to the attorney or representative for inspection. There is a contract and agreement dated

May 8, 1923, to obtain landing of a Chinese as a son of a native for the consideration of $2600 gold. This contract apparently refers to Yip Wo, admitted on appeal[1]. . . .

One is compelled to marvel at the extensiveness of coaching facilities. It appears evident that only persons thoroughly familiar with our procedure, with Department precedents and court decisions as to what constitute relevant points could have prepared the material included in these documents. One of the papers indicate a Chinese boy spent a year in one village so as to become conversant with conditions there and rumor has it that in China coaching classes are conducted in certain mercantile establishments, if not in some schools.

In handling Chinese cases one cannot but observe the untenable family claims of "all boys and practically no girls.". . .

The ratio of sixty-eight boys to three girls has never been attained among any race of people and clearly is impossible, yet that is approximately the ratio throughout our immigration records. During the fiscal year 1923 there were 2,437 Chinese applicants whose cases involved U.S. citizenship, and upon the premise of the foregoing computation the basis was laid for the admission of 6,921 U. S. citizens, of which number 6,228 are males and of these 5,403 are yet in China. Giving consideration to the numbers admitted at other ports and for all ports since the exclusion act became effective, it is a conservative figure to estimate that the foundation has been laid for the admission of at least 25,000 Chinese as U.S. citizens and the increase each succeeding year will be proportionate. The restriction placed upon alien Chinese will enhance the value of citizenship stati, will make the securing of same expensive and will tend to intensify and prolong coaching so as to forestall exclusion, which has the effect of breaking a U. S. citizenship chain, as it were. When exclusion does occur no funds are lacking to prosecute appeals to the Department and courts, it having been remarked the percentage of cases receiving favorable action warranted such action.

In the opinion of this office the present system and viewpoint of handling Chinese cases fosters the success of the fraudulent applications and even has the tendency to compel the legitimate applicant to resort to irregular practices to press his claims. However, while the foundation has been laid and a greater part of the super-structure is underway, the building is being weakened by the sands of fraud and should be further doomed by corrective legislation and regulations.

[1]Bureau file 55245/849, March 18, 1924, S. F. file 22753/5-12.

We would respectfully submit suggestions and recommendations for the consideration of the Bureau and Department as follows:

(1) Enactment of legislation which would deny U.S. citizenship status to foreign born children of U.S. citizens of the race that are ineligible to citizenship, providing for admission as the minor children as aliens if demanded as a humane measure by making it conditional upon both or the surviving parent being a lawful resident in the United States. While the present test is one of relationship conceded upon a showing of preponderance of evidence, it confers upon the applicant the highest possible privilege—that of citizenship, and this it accomplishes without the aid of white witnesses who are themselves U.S. citizens of good character but by the corroborative testimony of Chinese aliens, concerning whom no investigation is had and whose statements concern conditions in China impracticable of verification. It would be infinitely better to admit as aliens than to perpetuate U.S. citizenship stati.

(2) Cancel the rule which grants to Chinese the right of provisional denial. It is impossible under present conditions, and even unlikely under any condition, to prevent the sending and receiving of coaching letters by applicants in detention, as is evidenced by the numerous coaching letters included among the inclosures. The avenues are many and the price paid is a tempting inducement. One of Yip Sing's notations quotes $5 as the cost of one transaction. The provisional denial affords no other opportunity than time to compare testimony, to effect communications and coach additional witnesses. . . . There is no apparent reason why if care is exercised to see that sufficient time is allowed, all witnesses and evidence cannot be presented for consideration at the first hearing, leaving to the board of special inquiry the authority to defer final action should that body consider such action advisable. . . . This office believes that Chinese claiming U.S. citizenship should be treated as are other races, thus avoiding delays, detention expenses and the aiding of fraudulent transactions. . . .

(3) Cancel the instruction granting representatives of applicants claiming citizenship the loan of triplicate copy of testimony. These copies are being loaned to Chinese who make copies of same for coaching purposes. In the instant case the triplicate copy was found in Yip Sing's possession. One of our officers, when visiting a store to inspect the mercantile status, saw a Chinese in the act of copying a record. This office has reason to believe that every such record is copied before being returned. The flagrant abuse of this privilege is evident by the information in the hands of Yip Sing. . . .

(4) Members of boards of special inquiry and boards of review handling Chinese cases should be highly trained officers, inasmuch as they

are called upon to detect during the short period of a hearing the fraudulent cases which has been built up with the greatest of preparations and after months and even years of coaching. The undersigned found that a member of the inspectors at this port were of the opinion that the Bureau and Department demanded short hearings, having been so admonished by a Bureau representative who visited this port some years past. Where relationship claims involve U.S. citizenship, it is evident that a shortened hearing is an aid to coached cases since there would be fewer chances of disclosing discrepancies. There must of necessity be "fishing expeditions" in this class of cases to the end that sufficient material discrepancies can be adduced to offset the weight of the preponderance of evidence which has been established by court decisions. . . .

This office is convinced after several months of first hand observation that the present system is not conducive to the welfare of the government, nor in fact to the interest of the bona fide applicant, and that by gradual steps it has gotten more and more into a rut which becomes deeper and narrower as time goes on, making it more difficult and expensive for the government to detect the fraud and easier for the perpetration and success of irregular practices. Were the sole result that of testing the right of admission it would not become so vital a matter, but admission in these cases virtually confers U.S. citizenship with all the rights and privileges attending that honor and there is grave doubt that the duties of such citizenship have ever become inculcated upon the minds of such foreign born citizens. In fact, it would appear that the Oriental subserves the laws of this country, and in fact any law, whenever his own personal interests are an issue, and it is surprising to note the cleverness with which the Oriental interests prominent and influential citizens in their cases and sway such citizens to their viewpoint regardless of the adverse evidence before the officials of the government. . . .

The foregoing comments are made without prejudice to any race of people as it has been and will continue to be the policy of this office to enforce the law, regulations and instructions impartially to all and with a desire that the principle of right prevail.

We would urge adoption of the recommendations numbered 2, 3 and 4 until such time as there are changes in the law, and respectfully request the return of the original documents and photographs after having served the purpose of the Bureau and Department.

John D. Nagle
Commissioner.

21

EMERY SIMS

"Giving Every Applicant a Square Deal"

1929–1940

The son of immigrant parents from Canada, Emery Sims grew up in North Dakota before moving to San Francisco in 1929 to look for work. He started out as a stenographer at the Angel Island Immigration Station. Six years later, Sims was promoted to immigrant inspector after he passed the civil service exam with high marks. A diligent worker, he earned the reputation of being a "fair" inspector, one who believed in giving every applicant "a square deal." The following piece includes excerpts from an oral history interview that was conducted with Sims in 1977. He said then that he had not intended to stay long with the Immigration Service, but the work was so interesting, the hours short, and the pay good that he ended up putting in thirty years before he retired in 1957. A slim and soft-spoken man, Sims was eighty-five years old at the time of our interview and lived to be eighty-nine.

I moved to San Francisco when the big depression was coming on, and I just took any job that I could find. I started as a stenographer and was assigned to the record vault at Angel Island. There were masses of records of people from foreign countries, especially from China. My first job was to retrieve records from the vault.[1] You see, when Chinese or Japanese people came from the Orient and were detained, a file was started on that person with a file number made up of his ship's number and the page and line of the ship's manifest. Now suppose the ship had come to New York and there was a Chinese newcomer among the passengers. The New York office—then Ellis Island—would send out here for any records we might have on that person's relatives. My job

---

[1]The large fireproof vault was kept in the administration building and held close to 750,000 Chinese records in 1914. It survived the 1940 fire, which destroyed the administration building.

Emery Sims, interview with Judy Yung, Him Mark Lai, and Genny Lim, San Francisco, June 29, 1977. Interview #47, Angel Island Oral History Project, Ethnic Studies Library, University of California, Berkeley.

would be to go through the San Francisco records and pick out the file of the person's father or any brothers or sisters, bundle them up, and send them to New York. It was the same way with Boston, Philadelphia, Seattle, and Los Angeles. Large numbers of Chinese immigrants were arriving in New York and Boston at that time.

About 90 percent of our files were on the Chinese because we handled persons of Oriental descent—Chinese, Japanese, Indians or Hindus, and Filipinos. Some of the files were quite thick, since the Chinese were usually questioned at length when they first arrived. The Japanese were processed more quickly because they were mostly children who had been born here and had been taken to Japan for their education. It wasn't too hard to definitely identify them. Filipinos were rarely detained or interrogated because the Philippines was a part of the United States, so their status was different from other immigrants'.

At that time, a new arrival was held for a hearing before a Board of Special Inquiry, as we called it. That consisted of two inspectors, a stenographer, and an interpreter. The interpreter was not really on the board, but the other inspector and the stenographer had the privilege of asking questions if they desired. The inspector, to whom the case was assigned, was handed the file with any related files of that person's family. And then it was up to him to review these old files and start questioning the applicant about his birth, family, home, and in the course of the testimony, it would develop that the applicant was either very much in accord with the old files or there were rather serious discrepancies between him and the others. It was the only means we had, although it wasn't a very good method, because in a way, the Immigration Service built a way for them to be coached, to learn their testimony and get by. We just worked on the theory that this was the law and we had to carry it out. Some of the inspectors held prejudicial views against the Chinese and gave them a harder time during the hearing. I felt each one was entitled to a square deal, and I tried to give it to him as much as I could. In a way, the Chinese exclusion laws did touch me, and when they were repealed, I thought that was a good thing.

I remember that the interrogation rooms were bright, airy rooms. There would be the stenographer's desk and another desk or two. When the applicant was brought in, he would be given a seat where he could be at ease and talk as he wished and where the interpreter could communicate with him. Around 15 percent of the cases I handled were women. I don't remember any prostitutes, except one instance after World War II. There were many, many boys coming through—twelve, fourteen, fifteen years old, a lot of them smart kids. They were very sure of themselves. I've known of families of four or five coming together. They would question one briefly, just to a certain point, and the other one briefly just to a certain point. Then they would call back the first one and go a little further. That way, the family couldn't get together and talk about what had been said.

The testimony was taken directly on the typewriter in shorthand. Usually you would start with the immigrant himself and check his testimony against his relatives'. The applicant would be questioned about his birthday, about his parents, about his brothers and sisters, and about the village he lived in. That might be quite brief, or it might drag out with some inspectors to forty or fifty pages of typed testimony. Altogether, it could take from one to three or four days for him and the witnesses. If the testimonies matched, we had to give them the benefit of the doubt. A minor discrepancy would not carry much weight. If it was something serious . . . I remember a case of a boy whose father was bringing him in. He said his mother was so-and-so, but his father said the mother was so-and-so. Still the boy insisted she was so-and-so. Well, he didn't stay.

After the board heard the testimony, they would be pretty much in accord as to what was right and what was not. Any disagreement would mean a denial for the person. If two voted to land him and one voted to deny him, the dissenting member could appeal the case. But if he didn't wish to appeal, the person was landed. Then the file would be sent to the detention quarters with an order to land. If denied, the person was not notified until the testimony was all summed up, but he would be given that notice eventually. If the applicant wished to appeal, a copy of the testimony would be sent to the central office in Washington, D.C., and the attorney handling the case would be given a copy from which he made his appeal. Washington would probably make its decision based on the transcript alone.

More than 75 percent passed the interrogation at Angel Island and were released within two months of their arrival. There could have been indications of fraud in some of them, but nothing that would stand up in court to debar them. Of those who were denied entry, there was always an appeal to Washington, and probably only 5 percent of those who were denied were actually deported. Some who were deported came back and tried again, and made it. They knew you knew they were here before. If we found they were using another name, they could be excluded. All those deported had their photographs taken before they left. They were kept here and could be checked if the person returned.

The interpreters we had were pretty good on most of the dialects. We would use one interpreter with the applicant. Then when we had the witness, we would change interpreters. The inspector in charge had to rotate the interpreters, so the first interpreter might not be available for the recall. One time I asked one of our interpreters what percentage of cases was fraudulent. I asked if 90 percent were, and he said probably. I was aware of it from the beginning. I remember one case I was very sorry about. A father had brought a boy in when it was a daughter that he really had. She later came, and I forget how he brought it up that she was really his daughter, and she really was, but the boys that he had gotten paid for bringing in had spoiled things for her. She was deported, but she married a G.I. and later came back.

I know bribes did happen, but the cases were very rare. I don't think I ever had anything offered to me, but in a few cases, some of the others had. It was something that was hard to prove. I was aware that coaching notes were being sneaked in. The administration tried to prevent it by checking the mail. I heard of a capsule being put in a bowl of soup with a little note inside. They got the capsule but nothing developed from it. I know the kitchen help used to give them a lot of help, but there was nothing we could do about it. Overall, I found the law work interesting, and I enjoyed matching wits with the applicants. A lot of them had sharp minds.

22

EDWAR LEE

"Not a Ghost of a Chance for a Chinese to Be an Inspector"
1927–1938

Edwar Lee was born in San Francisco Chinatown in 1902. His father was an herb doctor, and his mother, a well-educated woman from Shanghai. Lee was a charter member of Troop Three, the first Chinese Boy Scout troop in the United States, and the first Chinese American to become a Methodist minister. He earned a BA from the College of the Pacific and a master's degree in political economics from the University

Edwar Lee, interview with Him Mark Lai, Genny Lim, Judy Yung, and Nelson Yee, Oakland, CA, May 8, 1976; interview with Felicia Lowe, Oakland, CA, April 9, 1984. Interview #50, Angel Island Oral History Project, Ethnic Studies Library, University of California, Berkeley.

of California, Berkeley. When racial discrimination prevented him from finding a job in his field, he went to work as a Chinese interpreter at the Angel Island Immigration Station. Lee resigned in 1938 to become the full-time pastor of the Oakland Chinese United Methodist Church. The following story about his experiences and insights as an immigration interpreter is based on two oral history interviews that were conducted with Lee in 1976 and 1984.

I had just graduated from UC Berkeley with a master's degree in political economics and was looking for a job. I tried several commercial firms without success. I was told either that the job had been filled or that it was against company policy to hire Orientals. Deaconess Katharine Maurer, whom I had befriended through my student pastor work at Chinese Methodist missions, asked if I would like to work for the Immigration Service, and I said yes, I'd give it a try. So she made an appointment for me to see the head inspector, Mr. P. B. Jones. I went over to Angel Island, met him for an interview, and was immediately hired. The main selection criterion at that time was one's competence in handling the different Chinese dialects. Having grown up in Chinatown and taught English to Chinese immigrants, I could converse in Sze Yup, Sam Yup, and the Chungshan dialects with ease. So that's how I landed the job as interpreter, not knowing that I would stay there for the next ten years. In those days, there wasn't a ghost of a chance for a Chinese to be an inspector, even if you had a very high education. I knew there was racial discrimination in the whole system, but I still felt that I could render a service to the government and to Chinese immigrants as well.

In the heyday, there were nine Chinese interpreters, and we all commuted. I was living in Berkeley. Every morning, I would walk two blocks to catch the train to the pier, take the ferry over to San Francisco, and walk over to Pier 5 to catch the 8:30 government cutter over to Angel Island. We would begin work at 9:00 or 10:00, take a lunch break, quit at 4:30, and get back to San Francisco by 5:00. We did that five days a week. It was a pretty good job. The starting salary was $130 per month, compared to $30 for Chinatown grocery clerks at the time. We weren't considered part of civil service until the 1930s, so we had no pensions and could be fired summarily. But we were given thirty days of sick leave. There was quite a bit of camaraderie among the interpreters, but very little between the interpreters and the inspectors for the obvious reason that we didn't want people to think we were in cahoots with them. All the years I was with the service, I never once attended their annual picnic.

No one interpreter sat throughout the same case. Because they were afraid of collusion between the interpreters and the applicants, they assigned one case to two or three interpreters. One interpreter would translate for the father, another one for the son, and another one for the mother. That could extend a case to one day, two days, or three days. The length of time all depended on whether the case was complicated or not. They would ask for names of relatives, how many houses in the village, different aspects of village life, what the applicant had been doing in China, and so on. Sometimes there was a contradiction between the father's and son's testimonies, and then they would have to call the father back from San Francisco. It depended also on the inspector, whether he was long-winded, drawn-out, and detailed. There were some inspectors who could, if they sensed something was wrong, get right on to it. They got through a case very fast. It took longer to take care of a doubleheader—a mother and son coming as newcomers—or tripleheader—three in the family. The father may already have had some sons over here, so the sons would serve as corroborating witnesses. Or sometimes a friend or fellow villager would be a witness. So you had to take testimonies from two or three persons representing the petitioner. Then you had to interrogate the applicant—one or two times or even more. If the only witness lived out of town, like in New York or Chicago, they took the testimony out of the New York office or the Chicago office. That's why it took a lot of time adjudicating some of these cases.

The applicants were all pretty young, because by the very nature of it, claiming to be sons and daughters of natives or merchants, you couldn't apply once you turned twenty-one. If it was a wife of a merchant, she could be any age. But nobody's going to bring in an old woman. During the interrogation, some were very calm and nonchalant. You asked a question, they answered. Then there were some who were very nervous, so I generally told them to just calm down and take their time answering. Some were a little hotheaded, with a chip on the shoulder. "Why should you ask me all these questions?" and so on. In general, I think it was remarkable that the applicants, kids and women, were rather stoical. They took it matter-of-factly, knowing that they could always appeal the case and finally be landed.

One time, a Chinese woman who was a prostitute applied for admission. She came over on first class. Because there was a "knocking letter"[1] filed against her, they detained her. Usually first-class passengers were landed from the boat. But they took her over to the island and gave

---

[1] An anonymous letter sent to immigration officials reporting a false claim.

her a very exhaustive examination. And this woman physically attacked the inspector. She was that angry with the number of questions asked of her and all the damaging evidence in the knocking letter. This was the only time in all the years I was there that I saw a Chinese woman attack an inspector. Needless to say, she was deported.

The interrogations were so tedious, in such minute detail, that you were bound to trip. Let me give you a humorous situation. I think it was a case of a triple-header. A mother and two kids came in at the same time, and a question by the inspector was: "Is there a dog in the house?" If you lived in the same house, you would know whether there's a dog or not, especially if the dog is your pet. So the mother said, "Yes, we have a dog." And another son, "Yes, we have a dog." And the third son, "No, no dog." So they called in the mother again, and the son, and they both said, "Yes, yes, we had a dog." And the other son was called in again. "Did you say that you have a dog in the house?" "Oh, we had a dog, but we ate that dog before we left. No dog!" Well, this was true. By the time he left home, there was no dog. Otherwise, it would be a very serious discrepancy if you lived in the same household and two said there's a dog and the other one said no.

The Board of Special Inquiry consisted of one inspector who was the chairman, a second inspector, and the stenographer who took down all the testimony and had decision-making power. The interpreter didn't count in the ruling. We just interpreted what the applicant said or what was asked. But we did render an opinion as to that person's dialect. Because if I said the son spoke in the Chungshan dialect and another interpreter said the father spoke in the Toishan dialect, immediately, the inspector would smell a rat. And then, of course, the inspector would also make a judgment as to family resemblance, and that went into the record. This was very important because the appeal was often based on the fact that there was a close resemblance.

Most of the time, the board was unanimous in their decision to land or deny admission into the country. Once in a long while, you would have a second member who disagreed with the chairman. At the end of the hearing, he would be allowed to state his reason for disagreeing. I remember one time a woman stenographer disagreed with the two inspectors and she was in tears arguing with the chairman. She thought that the inspectors had been rather prejudiced against the applicant, so she voted to dissent. So even the stenographer had the right to question the applicant and rule in the case, but we interpreters didn't have a voice whatsoever.

By and large, I think the inspectors were good people. Most were very fair-minded and impartial, like one old man, George Washington Kenney. He said, "I don't care if he is a fake. If he can pass my examination, he lands and good luck to him!" Well, that's fair. After all, he answered all the questions correctly. Then there were some who were very technical, very prejudiced, who had no love for the Chinese. They would go out of their way to trip you up and deny you admission. Working there day in and day out, and asking the same questions all the time, they got very impatient and irritable, and some were not as kind as they should've been toward these new immigrants.

I remember one case. Someone came on a birth certificate and landed. Another person came and claimed the same identity and that he was born in this country, but that his birth certificate had been stolen. He was denied admission, but Washington sustained his appeal on the grounds that he might've been the true one. The first one that came may have really stolen his paper. Then a third one came claiming the same thing, that the first two were false. So it was brought up to the U.S. District Court, and he was also landed. The court proceeded on the standpoint that no matter how many were fraudulent, one person was true, and it had not been proven that this third person was not true. So there was a certain amount of fairness in all this.

Surprisingly, I don't remember any breakdowns when detainees were told their case had been denied. But there was one case of suicide while I was there, over in the women's quarters. This woman was destined for Chicago. She brought in a real son and a ringer. It was clear in my mind that one of them was a ringer. So this woman, when told her case was denied, felt that the whole thing was washed up, that she might be deported back to China, a most terrible shame. So she sharpened a chopstick and stuck it in her brain through the ear. Died immediately. And even before Washington had a chance to deliberate on the case, the commissioner phoned Washington about the suicide. So promptly the word came, "Land them." So they landed the two sons.

I would say at least half of the cases were denied. Look at it this way. For each boat that arrived, you had ninety-five sons against one daughter. So you know that a lot of them were false. We might as well admit it. But 60 to 70 percent of the cases that were appealed to Washington were sustained, usually on the grounds that the questions were unfair or too prejudiced. That's before blood tests were done. It was just based on how well you did at the interrogation. If you passed, you were landed.[2]

---

[2]Based on statistical data from the National Archives, 9 percent of the Chinese applicants were rejected, 88 percent appealed their cases, 55 percent of the appeals were successful, and 7 percent were deported in the end. See Table 2 in Lai, Lim, and Yung, *Island*, 2nd ed., 342.

It didn't happen often, but I do remember a case or two of someone asking me to bribe the inspector, and I said, "Oh, no, no, no. Don't waste your money!" Sometimes it was very awkward when you were offered a bribe. You told them you didn't want the money, and they'd turn around and say it was because you felt it was too little, or they'd accuse you of being uncooperative and having no love for country or countryman. But we had to protect ourselves against accusations from applicants. It was generally the *bao wai*, the broker who took care of the case, who told them, "I have to give money to the inspector and the interpreter." But actually, he pocketed the money and just hoped the case would get through. If it didn't, he told them it was because the money wasn't enough.

I remember I once went to Gilroy to hear a case involving an herbalist who wanted to bring his wife in as a merchant's wife. So we had the hearing in his store. It was during wintertime and I had a big overcoat. I was in the store a long time, so I took my overcoat off and laid it on the counter. And he said, "I'll hang it up for you." So he took it to the back of the store and hung it up. When I left the store, I found this money in my pocket. Not much — $20, I remember. Well, I couldn't account for it and I couldn't tell the inspector that I had received this $20, because I would only jeopardize that case if I said so. But I never asked for the bribe. It was just tea money — they hoped you would put in a good word for them.

Our interpreting services were used in other situations, like scanning mail for coaching notes or investigating cases in the community. I remember once being asked to smooth things out after a food riot. You see, the concessionaire only received so much money from the steamship company to pay for the board of these people until they were released, sometimes for six weeks, two months, or even three months. So naturally, the company tried to pay as little as possible to the concessionaire to feed the people. This concessionaire then hired the Chinese staff and tried to think of the cheapest meal they could produce. Another problem was that the kitchen was designed for serving American food or large quantities for the army. So they had a lot of steamers instead of woks. You can imagine the difficult situation. No wok to cook Chinese food. And then they would buy the cheapest grade of rice and steam it in these big steamers. So the detainees got mad and started a riot. That's when they sent us in to calm everyone down.

There's no question in my mind that the Chinese immigrants who came through Angel Island went through quite an ordeal. It was a very harrowing experience for them to be cooped up in close quarters for long periods of time. Their cases usually didn't come up for a hearing for at least two weeks, and if they were denied, their wait on the appeal might take anywhere from three months to six months. And all that time, they were in a very sad situation. It was all because of the Chinese Exclusion Act. You'd think the government could think of a better way of handling these immigrants. But the inspectors by and large felt, "We didn't ask them to come to this country. They themselves applied for admission to this country, so it's only right that they prove they have a right to come into the country." On the part of the Chinese, they realized that while the immigration laws and policies discriminated against them, their chances of landing on final appeal were very good, so they were willing to put up with it. Actually, the present system is best. Why bring them over to this country, give them a hearing, and then deny them entry? Why go through all that heartache, expense, and everything else? Pre-determine the case in Hong Kong—that's the best solution.

23

JANN MON FONG

A Gold Mountain Man's Monologue

March 5, 1935

Jann Mon Fong (aka Smiley Jann) was born in Zhongshan District, Guangdong Province, in 1913. He completed eight years of schooling before he found a way to fulfill his dream of reaching Gold Mountain. He bought papers to immigrate as Sue Sow Fong, the son of a U.S. native. Upon arrival in San Francisco, Jann came to a rude awakening. His three-week confinement at Angel Island so angered him that he decided to write home about it. "I wanted my classmates to know that America is not as great as everyone thinks, that we actually suffered a great deal of humiliation," he said many years later in an interview.[1] His friends in Shanghai later submitted his essay, "A Gold Mountain Man's Monologue," to the journal, Renjian Shi *(People's World), for publication. It is a rare emotional and immediate first-hand account of how one*

---

[1]Smiley Jann, interview with Him Mark Lai and Judy Yung, San Francisco, January 4, 1976. Interview #32, Angel Island Oral History Project, Ethnic Studies Library, University of California, Berkeley.

Jann Mon Fong, "A Gold Mountain Man's Monologue," *Renjian Shi*, March 5, 1935, 15–16. Translated by Marlon K. Hom.

*Chinese immigrant responded to his imprisonment at Angel Island. It is
also one of the earliest publications of the Angel Island poems, as Jann
thought to include five of the ninety-nine poems he had copied off the
walls of the detention barracks into a notebook during his stay.*

*After he was released from Angel Island, Jann Mon Fong adopted the
name Smiley Jann and forged ahead with his life in America. He got
married, had four children, and ran a grocery store in San Francisco for
over thirty years. In 1959, he voluntarily participated in the Confession
Program and cleared his name so that he could become a U.S. citizen
and make periodic visits to China.[2] Smiley Jann passed away in 1997,
leaving behind his notebook of Angel Island poems, which he titled, "A
Collection of Autumn Grass: Voices from the Hearts of the Weak."[3]*

Whenever there was an air-horn-blasting, foreign steamship arriving at
port, there would be our countrymen among the passengers returning
home after striking it rich in foreign soil. Their suitcases were filled with
foreign dollars that would enable them to pursue all the comforts they
needed for their triumphant homecoming. They would also speak of the
sights and sounds of Gold Mountain and show off their riches. This was
indeed the envy of everyone. I, too, could not resist that envy and temp-
tation of wealth, and for some time had so wished for the opportunity to
go overseas.

Time passed, and without realizing it, I had become a young adult.
Money also became a desperately needed commodity in those years of
worldwide depression. My mind was preoccupied with the thought of
leaving home to seek a living. Three years ago, at the time of the summer solstice when apricots were ripening, I spent a huge sum of money
in silver dollars to buy a slot to come to America. By next summer when
the lychees were in season, I left home, bidding farewell to my beloved
parents.

It took only a few hours to get to Hong Kong from Chungshan. But
the U.S. consulate in Hong Kong dictated that all U.S.-bound Chinese
people must report at least half a month in advance for pre-departure
immunizations and the physical examination. It was done, as they said,
so that we would go to the wonderfully sanitized United States with

---

[2]According to the FBI investigation on June 2, 1959, Jann admitted to his fraudulent
entry in 1931 and named members of his paper family and his real family. After a brief
interview and a criminal background check, he was granted permanent residency as
Smiley Mon Fong Jann. See Alien File A11814436 (Sue Sow Fong), obtained via Freedom of Information Act request to the U.S. Citizenship and Immigration Services.

[3]A copy is available at the Ethnic Studies Library, University of California, Berkeley.

clean and healthy bodies, after clearing all the dirty and harmful substances inside our body system. For the sake of economic advancement in America, and like all my fellow countrymen, I subjected myself to this ridiculous process. Still, I didn't comprehend the implications behind it.

After braving the winds and waves for twenty days, the ship finally docked. The returning Gold Mountain old-timers left the pier soon after their immigration inspection. We, the newcomers, were transferred by a small boat to an island located inside the Golden Gate, which was, as told by old-timers, the immigration detention center for all incoming Chinese immigrants.

The moment we were put on the small boat, we lost all our freedom. The Americans treated us like cattle. Those green-eyed people must have thought Chinese were the offspring of pigs and goats. Carrying a cloth bundle on my back and a suitcase in my hand, I was herded into the detention center under their wolf-like authority. Tears flowed down my face. Fight back? Not a chance. How could I, since I had yet to learn their language upon arrival in their land?

First, we were put inside a small room surrounded with barbed wire. Their intention was obvious, but they claimed it had to be done as they reported our arrival to their superior officers. At that moment, I was saddened by the realization that my country and my people were powerless, and that I, myself, was facing an unknown and uncertain future. Now we went from being treated like a herd of cattle to being treated like hapless birds confined to a cage, ready for slaughter.

On that first day, we had breakfast before daybreak, and it wasn't until evening that we heard the call for supper. I didn't feel hungry all day, probably because I was full from being fed up with the cruel treatment there. Soon we were led into a huge prison. The moment we were all inside, they locked the door tightly. I found my bunk. Several fellow countrymen who had been detained there for some time asked me to join the Self-governing Association that had been established by the Chinese detainees. About two hundred of us detainees attended the meeting, during which the association officers told us the rules and regulations.

We were subject to yet another physical examination the next day, and the procedure, targeting our entire race, was particularly humiliating. The physician ordered us to disrobe and bear the chilly sea breeze for hours. He felt our chest and spine, and ordered us to jump around like monkeys. I was not sure if this was a physical examination, or, rather, an act of insult. Well, it was said that my treatment was actually light and easy. In the past, they would draw blood from our flesh to test for hookworm disease.

In the Self-governing Association office were a phonograph, some record albums, and fiction books. There was also a small playground

outside the detention barracks. Like the dormitory, it was also surrounded by barbed wire. The Caucasian guards kept the key to the
playground's gate. In fact, there were armed guards on patrol both
inside and outside the detention barracks.[4] Don't ever think of trying to
escape; they would send you off to another world. For the Chinese held
up there, there was little if any freedom accorded them!

All over the walls of the dormitory were numerous scribbling of
poems, rhymes, ditties, and parallel couplets written by Chinese detainees. Being idled there, I copied them down verbatim in a notebook without any editorial changes. Here are a few examples.

> May I advise you not to sneak across the barrier?
> Green waters surround a green hill on four sides.
> Ascending to a high place, one does not see the shore.
> To cross the green waters is the most difficult of difficulties.

> Life is worth worrying about, and you should restrain yourselves.
> Do not treat these words as idle words.
> Why not let them send you back to China?
> You will find some work and eke out a couple of meals.[5]

*   *   *

> It is indeed pitiable, the harsh treatment of our fellow countrymen.
> The doctor extracting blood caused us the greatest anguish.
> Our stomachs are full of grievances, but to whom can we tell them?
> We can but pace to and fro, scratch our heads, and question the
>   blue heavens.[6]

*   *   *

> Flocks of fellow villagers do not refrain from spending thousands
>   of gold pieces to get to America.
> Several hundred compatriots invested huge sums but are now
>   imprisoned on Island.[7]

*   *   *

---

[4]As a rule, guards did not carry weapons at the immigration station except during a
period in the 1930s when federal prisoners were temporarily housed there.

[5]Poem 128 in Lai, Lim, and Yung, *Island*, 2nd ed., 156.

[6]Poem 94, Lai, Lim, and Yung, *Island*, 2nd ed. 126.

[7]Poem 16, Lai, Lim, and Yung, *Island*, 2nd ed. 58.

Random Thoughts on the Island[8]

Drifting alone in the ocean, autumn suddenly passed.

I have just gone through ten thousand calamities; still I am a prisoner from Chu.[9]

When Wu Zixu played his flute, he thought of erasing his grievances.[10]

When Su Ziqing held his tasseled staff, he vowed he would one day avenge his wrongs.[11]

When Jiyun shot an arrow at the enemy, he was not doing it to meddle.[12]

When Goujian slept on firewood, he had a reason.[13]

My inflamed liver and bowels are prepared to take life lightly and engage in a life-and-death struggle.

Will the blue heavens allow me to fulfill this ambition or not?

* * *

This unworthy one with the group is grief-stricken.

Who will transmit the news of death back to the village?

I mourn your having ridden the crane to return to the dark regions.[14]

A traveler arrived in America on a ship.

Tears enveloped the lonely soul as the cuckoo uttered its mournful cry.

[8]Poem 83, Lai, Lim, and Yung, *Island*, 2nd ed. 114.

[9]A prisoner or a person in difficult straits.

[10]Wu Yun (d. 485 BCE), or Wu Zixu, was the son of a high official serving the King of Chu (a state in the central Yanzi River basin). His father fell into disfavor with the king and was killed together with his family. Wu Zixu, however, fled to the state of Wu (in present-day Jiangsu). He arrived with only a flute, which he played in the marketplace to beg for food. Later, he became an important official who served the Wu king and led an army to defeat the state of Chu. His victorious legions entered the Chu capital in 506 BCE, whereupon he dug up the corpse of the former king and whipped it three hundred times.

[11]Another name for Su Wu (140–60 BCE), who, during the Western Han dynasty (206 BCE–24 CE), was sent by the Chinese government as envoy to the Xiongnu, a nomadic people north of the Chinese empire. Su Wu was detained there for nineteen years but refused to renounce his loyalty to the Han emperor.

[12]Nan Jiyun (d. 757). During the An Lushan Rebellion, the rebel army surrounded Suiyang (in present-day Henan). Nan was one of the defenders of the besieged city and shot the enemy general in the left eye with one arrow.

[13]Goujian was king of the state of Yue (in present-day Zhejiang). In 494 BCE, he was ignominiously defeated by King Fucha's armies from the state of Wu. Yue recovered, and, two decades later, in 476 BCE, he returned to defeat Wu. It was alleged that King Goujian slept on firewood and tasted gall bladder in order not to forget the bitterness and humiliation of his defeat. Fan Li (Taozhugong) was one of his important ministers.

[14]Death. In Chinese mythology, cranes are connected with immortality.

Sorrow has led me to dream of traveling to the Terrace of Yang.[15]
It is a pity that medicine was wrongly prescribed.
The corpse was nearly cremated to ashes.[16]

These writings are the testimonies of hardship on their journey to America. Among these writings are references to suicides due to frustration and humiliation. As I was copying them from the walls, I was overwhelmed with grief and sorrow. I wrote the following in response to what I saw on the walls.

When I left, my parents regretted it was so hurried.
The reason I tearfully swallow my resentment is because of poverty.
Wishing to escape permanent poverty, I fled overseas.
Who caused my destiny to be so perverse that I would become imprisoned?
Victims of aggression, the people of our nation mourn the desperate times.
I feel sorely guilty for having not yet repaid my parents' kindness.
The chirping insects moan in the cold night.
Not only do I sob silently, but my throat tastes bitter.[17]

Altogether I spent twenty days in detention at the wooden barracks, two of which were for interrogation and deposition.[18] On the afternoon of the twentieth day, I was ferried out, and I finally landed in this place erroneously called since my childhood years the heavenly "Gold Mountain."

Perhaps we should think this over: We are dealt all this difficulty and adversity when going to another's country. Yet, when they come to our country, why do they behave so superior on our home soil?

[15]King Huai of Chu (328–299 BCE) met a female immortal in a dream and had sexual relations with her. She was found every morning and evening at the foot of the Terrace of Yang, which has come to be used as an allusion to a place where men and women meet for sex.

[16]Poem 111 in Lai, Lim, and Yung, *Island*, 2nd ed., 140.

[17]Poem 18, Lai, Lim, and Yung, *Island*, 2nd ed. 60.

[18]According to Jann's Alien File, his alleged father, alleged sister, and he were thoroughly investigated. They were interrogated for days and asked a total of 455 questions about their family background and the layouts of their house and village. Jann was able to answer all their questions with confidence, even as to how many children his mother's younger brother had, what were the floors in their house made of, when his sister started bobbing her hair, and whether his mother had any gold in her teeth. The summary report indicated that their testimonies were in "good agreement" and each of them had shown "excellent demeanor" throughout the examination. See Alien File A11814436 (Sue Sow Fong), obtained via Freedom of Information Act request to the U.S. Citizenship and Immigration Services.

24

LEE PUEY YOU

"A Bowlful of Tears"
1939–1940

Born in Zhongshan District, Guangdong Province, Lee Puey You was twenty-three years old when she immigrated to the United States in 1939 as Ngim Ah Oy, the "paper daughter" of a U.S. citizen. Once admitted, she was to marry a Chinese immigrant thirty years her senior in order to prepare the way for the rest of her family to come. Lee had expected to be detained at Angel Island for a few weeks, until she successfully passed the physical examination and interrogation. However, because of discrepancies in her testimony and in those of her witnesses, she was denied entry.[1] Her appeal went all the way to the U.S. Supreme Court, without success. After twenty months of confinement at Angel Island, she was deported to Hong Kong in the middle of the Sino-Japanese War. In 1947, she returned to the United States, posing as a war bride, to marry the same man. This time, she was admitted immediately. But the twenty months of prison-like detainment at Angel Island had been forever etched into her mind and heart. The following story, told in Lee Puey You's own words and translated into English, is drawn from two oral history interviews conducted with her in 1975 and 1984.

I didn't want to come to America, but I was forced by circumstances to come. When I was very young, my father was a wealthy farmer. A flood destroyed all his land and he lost all his money. It was then that our family's fortune changed. My father died and my brother had to go to work to support my mother and me. I saw how hard he worked, just one job. It was barely enough. So my mother arranged a marriage for me. I had a passport to come when I was sixteen, but I didn't come until I was twenty-three, after the Japanese attacked China. They bombed Shekki

---

[1]See transcript of hearing, Document 25.

Lee Puey You, interview with Him Mark Lai and Judy Yung, San Francisco, December 14, 1975; and interview with Felicia Lowe, San Francisco, April 11, 1984, Interview #11, Angel Island Oral History Project, Ethnic Studies Library, University of California, Berkeley.

and everywhere, and there was nowhere to hide so I had to come to America. But my fate was not good. I had never seen my fiancé before, but I knew he was a lot older than me. He said he would give me the choice of marrying him or not after I arrived. My mother wanted me to come to America so that I could help bring my brother and the rest of the family over later. Because of that, I was afraid to oppose the arranged marriage. I had to be a filial daughter. The situation forced me to sacrifice everything to come to America.

In 1939, I arrived at Angel Island. They told us to store our luggage in the shed, and then they directed us to the wooden building. We were allowed to bring only a small suitcase of clothes. The next day, we had to take a physical examination. When the doctor came, I had to take off all my clothes. It was so embarrassing and shameful. I didn't really want to let him examine me, but I had no choice. Back in China, I never had to take off everything, but it was different here in America. I found it very disturbing.

There must have been more than one hundred people detained on Angel Island. The men had their dormitories and the women had theirs. They assigned us to beds, and there were *gwai poh* [female foreign devils] to take care of us. Every day we got up at about 7:00. They yelled, "Chow, chow!" They would wake us up and take us to the dining room for breakfast—usually a plate of vegetables and a plate of meat catering to the Chinese palate. Sometimes scrambled eggs, sometimes vegetables mixed with meat. Their food was pretty bad, not very tasty. But then most people didn't eat their food. Many had relatives in the city who sent them Chinese dishes—barbecued duck and sausages, packages of food every day. After we ate, they took us back and locked the doors. That's all. Just like in jail. Followed us out and followed us back, then locked the doors. They treated us like criminals! They were always afraid that we would go over to the men's side and talk to them or that we might escape or commit suicide. Where would we escape to? I never saw anyone attempt suicide, but people did cry to die because they were suffering so.

There was really nowhere to go. Just a little breezeway that was fenced in for us to sun, exercise, or play ball. There was a long table for us to use for writing or sewing. From the windows we could see the boats arrive daily at about 9:30 or 10:00 in the morning. At the end of the day, we would watch the inspectors and newly released immigrants leave the island on the same boat. That's all. We couldn't have any visitors, but there was a Miss [Katharine] Maurer, a churchwoman who came once or twice a week. She was very nice to me, bringing me yarn or fabric. Sometimes I read or knitted, made some clothes, or slept. When you got up, it was time to eat again. Day in and day out, eat and sleep. It was hard, and time went by so slowly.

We had a bed to sleep in and the bathrooms were adequate, but it was noisy with so many people—fifty or sixty women at one time and a few young children besides. Sometimes the people next to you talked or people would cry in the middle of the night so you couldn't sleep. Sometimes people didn't get along and argued, but because we were in the same fix, we were generally good friends. We shared food and helped each other out even though I couldn't understand the Sze Yup dialect.[2] Often, those who had been there awhile cried when they saw others leave. So much mental anguish; we all suffered emotionally. No one had any energy. You know, sitting at Angel Island, I must have cried a bowlful of tears. It was so pitiful.

When I was in China, I didn't know it would be so hard in America. Everybody said that coming to America was like going to heaven, but at Angel Island they treated the Chinese as if we were all thieves and robbers. The bathroom was filled with poems expressing sadness and bitterness.[3] They were about how hard the stay at Angel Island was, how sad and depressed the women were, not knowing when they would be allowed to leave the island. Sometimes I wrote poems to console myself. That helped to release some of the tension. I would write and cry at the same time. During one of my more painful moments, I wrote this poem:

> Crossing the faraway ocean to arrive in America,
> Leaving behind my hometown, family, and friends—
> Who would have expected to be stranded in a wooden building,
> Not knowing when I can hold my head up with pride?[4]

In my darkest moment of sadness, I could only turn to God for help. I just prayed every day. That was the only way I could bear those hardships. I had no choice but to be strong. I had to take care of myself so that I might survive. I had to fulfill my duty as a filial daughter. That was all!

Two or three weeks after my arrival, I was called in for the interrogation. I knew I would be interrogated, but I was still nervous when the time came. There was a typist, an inspector, and an interpreter—three

---

[2] Most of the women were from the Sze Yup districts (Xinhui, Taishan, Kaiping, and Enping) in Guangdong Province, while Lee Puey You was from an area in Zhongshan District, where the Longdu dialect was spoken.

[3] Because a fire destroyed the administration building where Chinese women were kept, none of the women's poems have been preserved.

[4] Translated by Marlon K. Hom.

in all. Just looking at them made me scared. It went on for three days. We started at 9:30 or 10:00 in the morning. At 11:30 or 12:00 there was a lunch break. Then we went back at 1:00 until 4:00. They asked me about my grandparents, which direction the house faced, which house I lived in, how far from one place to another. It took a long time because after they asked me questions, they would ask my father, then my uncle, and then the two witnesses. That's why it took so long. Sometimes the interpreters were cranky. When I said I wasn't sure or I didn't know, they would tell me to say yes or no. They just treated us like criminals!

After the interrogation, if you failed, they didn't tell you. But when you were allowed to see your father or witnesses, you knew they were going to deport you. You see, if I had passed, I won't have had to see the witnesses. I would have been immediately called to land, to gather my things and leave. That's how it usually was. Relatives later told me that they would appeal my case to the higher authorities in Washington, D.C. They told me to be patient. My appeal failed the first time and then a second time. They were hoping that when the United States finally entered the war, I would be released. But instead, I was stuck on Angel Island for twenty months. I was there the longest. Most people stayed three weeks or so. Those on appeal left after a few months. But my case was more "crooked" because my paper father had not reported earlier that I was a twin, and I didn't know that. So I wasn't landed.

That was the system then, and there was nothing you could do about it. But this is how I look at it now. If things checked out at the American consulate in Hong Kong, they should let us come. If not, they shouldn't let us come. That would have spared us suffering twenty days aboard ship, seasickness and all, and then imprisonment at Angel Island. In my case, I had to endure twenty months of prison-like confinement. And then to be deported to Hong Kong, how sad!

During my trip back to China on the boat, my heart felt very heavy. I had "no face" to see my family. My spirit was broken. I finally had to put some rice, some hot rice, against my chest to ease the pain inside. The anguish that I had suffered is more than anyone can bear. I can't begin to describe it. Then all of a sudden, I had a dream. My appeal was successful! It was like a message from God. Then my heart was at peace. So that's my story from start to finish. It took me fourteen years to come back to America, fourteen long, long years.

As for my life in America, as long as you are willing to work hard, you can make a better living in America than in China. We had a grocery store, and since there were enough people working in the store, I was not needed. Later on, after my father-in-law passed away, that left only my husband and me to run the store. I would work every day from 7:00 a.m. to 9:00 p.m., fourteen hours a day, seven days a week. But I only did that for five or six years. Now my life is quite settled. I saved enough money to buy a building so that I can live in one apartment and rent the rest of the units out. I should be able to take care of myself for the rest of my life.

My mother had wanted me to come to America, hoping that later on I would somehow bring the rest of the family over. Twenty years later, my mother, my brother, his wife and their four children, my sister and her husband and children all came to America on a ship. It cost me thousands of dollars, but my mother's hopes have finally been fulfilled! Now all of them are doing well. They all have good jobs and their own homes. All the children have finished college and are making good money. Everyone is happy and my responsibility to them is finally over.

25

Lee Puey You's Interrogation
April 24, 1939

As the transcript of her interrogation shows, Lee Puey You's case was more complicated and drawn out than most other Chinese cases appearing before the Board of Special Inquiry at Angel Island. She was interrogated four times and each of her five witnesses at least twice while most other applicants were interrogated once or twice and usually only had one or two witnesses. Lee's case file amounted to fifty-four pages of testimony and six pages of the Board's summary judgement as compared to the average of twenty pages of testimony plus a one-page summary. The following excerpts from Lee Puey You's interrogation and the Board's summation point to the poor preparation of the applicant and witnesses, and the thoroughness of immigration inspectors in the cross-examination process. They had strong reasons for denying Lee Puey You entry into the country.

File 39071/12-9 (Ngim Ah Oy), 1–11, 31, 41–46, 48–53, Immigration Arrival Investigation Case Files, RG 85, National Archives, San Francisco.

RECORD OF BOARD OF SPECIAL INQUIRY HEARING

U.S. DEPARTMENT OF LABOR
Immigration and Naturalization Service
San Francisco, Calif.

Manifest No. 39071/12-9   Date: April 24, 1939

In the matter of: NGIM AH OY
Daughter of Son of Native
SS Pres. Pierce 4-13-39

At a meeting of a Board of Special Inquiry held at Angel Island
Present: Inspectors: M. A. Moore, Chairman
                              A. S. Hemstreet, Member
              Clerk: L. C. Sanderhoff, Member
              Interpreter: H. K. Tang.

Q. Have you ever been married? A. No.
Q. Of what country do you claim to be a citizen? A. The UNITED STATES.
Q. How do you believe that you acquired U.S. citizenship? A. My father
   was a U.S. citizen.
Q. Who is your father? A. NGIM LIN or NGIM CHUNG SUNG.
Q. Are you a blood child of NGIM LIN? A. Yes.
Q. How do you know that you are? A. Because he has been sending
   money to us.
Q. He might send money to you if you were his adopted child, or step-
   child or even a distant relative of yours. A. My mother told me that I
   am his blood daughter.
Q. What is your age according to Chinese reckoning? A. 22.
Q. What is your birth date according to the Chinese calendar? A. CR
   4-11-27 (Jan. 2, 1916), according to the old calendar.
Q. What year is this according to the Chinese calendar? A. Chinese
   Republic 28.
Q. How do you figure that you are now 22 years old by Chinese calen-
   dar? A. Wait, wait, let me try to think. I cannot figure it out.
Q. Do you always compute your age in accordance with western reckon-
   ing? A. Yes.
Q. Tell us how it happens that you do that if you always lived in CHINA?
   A. My mother told me that I was born according to the western cal-
   endar in CR 5-1-2 and that according to the old calendar I was born in
   CR 4-11-27. That is what I heard from my mother.

Q. How old is your mother? A. 41.

Q. Do you state her age also according to western reckoning? A. I heard that she was born in KS 25-4-8, old calendar. (May 17, 1899).

Q. Do you state your mother's age according to western or Chinese reckoning? A. According to the old calendar.

Q. What is your mother's age according to the new calendar, or the system by which you compute your own age? A. I do not know because she gave her age according to the old calendar.

Q. It seems very strange to us that you know your own age only according to American reckoning and your mother's age only according to Chinese reckoning. Do you wish to offer any explanation? A. No.

Q. In that case, you are informed that we must conclude that you have learned of your own claimed age from coaching matter. Have you any comment? A. I did not learn it from coaching papers.

Q. Then why don't you know your own age according to Chinese reckoning if you have lived with your mother who computes her age by Chinese reckoning? A. (after pause of several minutes during which applicant counts on her fingers) I am 24, Chinese reckoning.

Q. How did you first learn the date of your birth according to the Chinese calendar? A. My mother told me that when I was small.

Q. Have you ever seen your father? A. No.

Q. How many wives has your father ever had? A. Just one — my mother.

Q When were your parents married? A. I don't know.

Q. Have you any photograph of your mother? A. No.

Q. Did you ever see a photograph of your mother? A. No.

Q. How does your mother compare with you in size? A. My mother is a medium size woman.

Q. You do not answer the question. What we want to know is how you and your mother compare in size. A. I cannot answer your question because my mother is a woman neither tall nor short, neither stout nor slender.

Q. Your replies to these questions indicate to us that you are merely repeating what you have learned from coaching matter, and that you have never seen the woman whom you claim to be your mother. This board must conclude that that is the case unless you are able to give a more responsive and intelligent answer to this question. What do you wish to say? A. Well, I mean to say that my mother was about my size and my height.

Q. Is your mother fully as tall as you are? A. Yes.

Q. Does your mother resemble you? A. No, she does not look very much like me, although the size of her face is about the same as mine.

Q. Is your mother's complexion lighter or darker than yours? A. I am a little lighter than she.

Q. Were your mother's feet ever bound? A. No.

Q. Are your mother's ears pierced? A. Yes.

Q. How many children have your parents ever had? A. One twin brother, and no sisters of mine.

Q. Is your brother living? A. Yes.

Q. Describe him. A. NGIM JUNG HON, same as my age, and born on the same day I was.

Q. What is your brother's age? A. 23.

Q. Who is the older as between you and your brother? A. I am the oldest.

Q. Has your brother been known by any name other than NGIM JUNG HON? A. Yes, he is also known as MA NGEE. (meaning twin number two).

APPLICANT VOLUNTEERS: I am 22 years old by old reckoning; I made a mistake before.

Q. How do you know that you are now 22 years old by Chinese old reckoning? A. I just figured it out myself, but I do not know whether that is right or not. I just heard my mother say that I was born in CR 4-11-27, old calendar and in CR 5-1-2, western calendar.

Q. What is your brother's age according to Chinese reckoning? A. 22.

Q. Are you now certain that both you and your brother are 22 years old by Chinese reckoning? A. Yes.

Q. According to our records your alleged father could not have a legitimate child who is now 22 years old by Chinese reckoning. Have you any comment? A. But he has.

Q. Has your mother been in the U.S.? A. No.

Q. Inasmuch as your alleged father last left CHINA over 24 years ago, will you please explain how he could have a legitimate blood child who is now only 22 years old by Chinese reckoning? A. I want you to look it up carefully. My father has not returned to this country so long ago.

Q. Then when did your father last return to this country? A. I have never heard my mother say when my father came to this country.

Q. On what do you base your assertion that it has not been over 24 years since your father last left CHINA? A. Well, if my father has been there so long where could I have come from?

Q. That is just what we are inquiring into, and you are again reminded that the law places the burden upon you of proving your right to admission to the U.S. Now, do you wish to make any further statement in this connection? A. Perhaps I made a mistake in saying that I was 22 years old.

Q. Do you know how old you are? A. No, I really don't know my true age.

Q. Do you know the true age of your brother? A. My brother is 23 years old, same age as mine.

Q. How much older than your brother are you? A. I heard my mother say that I was born 3 or 4 minutes before my brother was.

Q. Does your brother closely resemble you? A. Not very much.

Q. Why is that if you are really twins? A. He looks somewhat like me, but I am a little taller than he.

Q. Is your brother stout or slender in build? A. He is of medium build.

Q. Have you any picture of your brother? A. No.

Q. Has he ever been photographed to your knowledge? A. No.

Q. Why is it that you are being brought here while your brother is left in CHINA? A. Because he has been attending school in CANTON CITY and his present whereabouts are unknown due to war conditions there. He went to CANTON CITY to attend school in CR 20 (1931).

Q. How long has it been since you or your mother has had word from or about your brother? A. My mother last received a letter from him about two years ago.

Q. How long has it been since you last saw your brother? A. I have not seen him since he lef home in CR 20 (1931).

Q. Who has been paying his expenses while he was attending school in CANTON CITY? A. I heard that his expenses have been supplied by my father and my maternal uncle WHOE TONG. They sent him the money for his expenses.

Q. Where did you learn that? A. I heard it from my mother.

Q. Has your brother ever been known as NGIM TAI (BAI)? A. No.

Q. Have you ever been known as NGIM YEE (NGEE)? A. No.

Q. In the latter part of the year CR 5 (1916) your alleged father testified that he had only one child, a son, that he had no daughter, and that his son's name was NGIM TAI and that he was born CR 4-10-29 (Dec. 5, 1913). How do you account for such a statement in view of your representations at this time? A. What my father said then is not true.

Q. Do you know of any reason he might have had at that time for denying that he had a daughter if it were true that he did have a daughter? A. He did not say that.

Q. Who do you think did say that on the occasion about which you have been informed? A. I cannot explain it. He must have a daughter otherwise he would not ask me to come at this time.

Q. The point we make is that when your alleged father gave this testimony which was on CR 5-9-7 (Oct. 3, 1916) he obviously did not have any daughter, and he could not have any legitimate blood daughter born to him subsequently. Do you wish to comment about that? A. Well, if I am not his daughter, why should he ask me to come.

Q. If it is true, as your alleged father stated under oath in CR 5-9 (Oct., 1916) that he had a son born to his wife on CR 4-10-29 how could his wife have two more blood children born to her on CR 4-11-27 as you claim? A. That is not true. I still ask you to look into it more carefully.

Q. As late as CR 11 (1922) your alleged father testified that his son was named NGIM TAI and his daughter NGIM NGEE. Have you any comment about that? A. That is not true. My name is DAI.

Q. Our records show that on three separate occasions your alleged father has claimed a son named NGIM TAI, and as you have already been informed, he originally claimed that this was the only child he ever had. Why should he make those repeated statements over a period of several years if he had no son named NGIM TAI but did have a daughter of that name? A. That is not true. I am DAI.

Q. Has your brother ever been married? A. No.

Q. How do you know that he hasn't if you have not heard from him for some years? A. He has been attending school. How could he have gotten married if he was attending school?

Q. How do you know that he has been attending school during the last few years if you have not heard from him? A. I do not know.

Q. Are your father's parents living? A. I heard that they are living in HOW CHUNG village, NOM LONG section.

Q. About when was it that you last heard that and what was the source of that information? A. I heard it from my mother from time to time.

Q. Did your mother tell you how she learned from time to time that your father's parents were both still living? A. She heard it from other people.

Q. Have you ever seen either of your paternal grandparents? A. No.

Q. What are their names? A. I heard his name — my grandfather's — is NGIM GAI or NGIM CHUN NAM. I also heard that his wife's name is LOW SHEE.

Q. Have you ever seen pictures of either of your paternal grandparents? A. No.

Q. Has your father ever had any brothers or sisters? A. I heard that he has 4 brothers and one sister.

Q. What are their names, ages, and whereabouts? A. I heard that their names are:

NGIN TIN, brother
NGIN HIN, brother
NGIN CHUNG MEE, brother
NGIN CHUNG JOW, brother
NGIN LAI CHOY, sister.

I heard my mother say that my paternal grandparents had brought them back to the HOW CHUNG village, but I have never seen any of them, and I don't know their ages. They are all younger than my father.

Q. Do you know if any of your father's brothers or his sister are now in this country? A. I don't know, but I heard my mother say that she had heard my father's sister was married to LUM BING FOON in the United States.

Q. Do you know anything regarding a family of any of your father's brothers or of his sister? A. No, I have never heard of any family.

Q. What were the names of your paternal great grandparents? A. I do not know. I never heard of any.

Q. Has your paternal grandfather any brothers or sisters? A. I do not know. I have never heard of any.

Q. Are your mother's parents living? A. No, they died a long time ago.

Q. What were their names and when did each of them die? A. I heard my mother's father's name is WOO HOOK and that he died a long time ago. His married name is WOO HUNG BUN. My mother's mother is YEE SHEE, who died before my mother was married to my father. My mother's father married three times, but all his wives are dead now.

Q. Are your mother and the witness WHOE TONG both children of the same mother? A. No. They have the same father but different mothers.

Q. Have you understood the interpreter? (through Edwar Lee) A. Yes.
TO INTERPRETER H. K. TANG:
Q. In what dialect has the applicant testified? A. HEUNG SHAN.

SIGNATURE OF APPLICANT: (in Chinese)

APPLICANT DISMISSED. . . .

SUMMARY BY CHAIRMAN
May 5th, 1939

<u>Name of applicant</u>: NGIM AH OY
<u>Status claimed</u>: Daughter of Son of Native
<u>Claimed age</u> (Am. Reckoning): 23 yrs., 4 mos.
<u>Birthdate claimed</u>: Jan. 2, 1916
<u>Previous appearances of applicant before this Service, if any</u>: NONE KNOWN

Witnesses:	Relevant trips of witnesses:
NGIM LIN, al. father—	1st arr. 5-3-15. No trips.
NGIM TIN, al. uncle (paternal)	1st arr. 1-1-09. Trips not relevant.
WHOE TONG, al. uncle (maternal)	none
LAU WAI YEE, id. witness—	1st arr. 10-17-33. No trips.
YOUNG MUEY, id. witness—	Dep. 2-5-38; ret. 5-24-38.

DISCUSSION OF EVIDENCE, and NOTICE.

It is claimed that this applicant derives United States citizenship through her alleged father, from NGIM CHUN KAM, whose American nativity and citizenship have often been conceded by this Service. For reasons which will be discussed herein, it is the opinion of this board that the claim that NGIM LIN is a son of NGIM CHUN NAM is false, and that recognition of that claim as a valid one by this Service has heretofore been accomplished by fraud and misrepresentation. We accordingly do not concede NGIM LIN's United States citizenship in the present matter. . . . A factor that is of the utmost importance and which appears to have been overlooked until the present time is the matter of the claimed ages and birthdates of LIN and TIN which precludes the possibility that both of these persons are blood children of NGIM CHUN NAM and his wife. . . .

None of the witnesses who claim to be related to the applicant has ever seen her, and it is claimed that neither the father nor the paternal uncle has ever been in the village in which it is claimed applicant has lived since she was about one month old. Each of the female witnesses is alleged to have met the applicant the customary two times in China. The situation here does not offer much of a field for examination and cross-examination along the usual lines. As between the applicant on one hand and her witnesses on the other, the statements agree substantially, although there are many indications, particularly in the applicant's testimony, that the story advanced is largely a fabricated one. Present testimony of NGIM LIN is not in accord with prior testimony given by himself, his alleged relatives, nor with the present statements of his alleged brother who has been introduced as a witness. It is also at varience with facts of which are of record in our files. The character of these discrepancies afford clear proof that the alleged father's claim of American citizenship is based upon fraud, and that he falsely claims the applicant to be his legitimate blood child. . . .

The alleged father makes two significant statements (pages 20 and 21) when he says, first, that he departed from China on May 23, 1915, and that he then knew that his wife was one or two months advanced in pregnancy. The fact is that he arrived at this port on May 3, 1915, and sailed from HONG KONG on April 6, 1915. He says that he left his wife in the home village and that it was a few days after he left the village that he sailed from HONG KONG. In other words, it was at the very least a full nine calendar months from the time he left his home in China to the time now asserted for the birth of the two children he now claims. If, as he says, he knew his wife to be one or two months pregnant before he left home, it would mean that the claimed children were not born until at least ten or eleven months after conception. We recognize, of course, that such a period of gestation is within the realm of possibility, but what we regard as the important point here is the obvious indication that the birthdate claimed is simply a fabrication built upon the alleged father's calculations on the basis of his mistaken belief that he had departed from China on May 23, 1915.

While this applicant has correctly stated her age as twenty-three years by our reckoning, she insisted (page 4) that she is only twenty-two years old by Chinese reckoning, until she was informed that she could not be the blood daughter of NGIM LIN and his wife if she is but twenty-two years old by Chinese count, whereupon she said that she might be mistaken in this regard. If she is in fact twenty-two years of age by Chinese reckoning, she was born in the year CR 7 (1918). . . .

It is our opinion that the evidence now before the government proves affirmatively that NGIM LIN is not the son of NGIM CHUN NAM, and that the evidence fails reasonably to establish that the applicant is the legitimate, blood child of NGIM LIN, as claimed. There is no other basis on which it is claimed the applicant is admissible, and I therefore move that she be denied admission into the United States, on the grounds —

That she is an alien Chinese person subject to exclusion under the Act of May 6, 1882, as amended, who does not possess the Certificate required by said Act; That she is an alien ineligible to citizenship who is not exempted from exclusion under any provision of

Section 13 (c) of the Immigration Act of 1924; and That she has failed to sustain the burden of proof, as required by Section 23 of the Immigration Act of 1924.

BY MEMBER HEMSTREET: I second the motion.
BY MEMBER HEADBERG: I concur.

26

Lee Puey You's Appeal
August 15, 1955

In 2000, while working on another article about Lee Puey You, I came to a different understanding of her immigration history and life in America. It had not been as "easy" as she had said. By then, Lee had passed away after a heroic battle against cancer, and I turned to her daughters, Daisy and Debbie Gin, for help in clarifying some discrepancies in her interview. Based on the immigration and court files that they found at the National Archives and through a Freedom of Information Act request, I learned that in 1955, someone blew the whistle and reported her illegal entry to the Immigration and Nationality Services (INS). A warrant for her arrest was issued on the grounds that the immigration visa she had used to enter the country in 1947 had been procured by fraud. She was ordered to appear before the INS in San Francisco to show cause as to why she should not be deported. The stakes were just as high as they had been for her at Angel Island in 1939.

The following excerpt is from Lee Puey You's hearing before the INS. Her declaration of innocence initially fell on deaf ears, and she was ordered to be deported on grounds that her immigration visa had been procured by fraud and that she was not a person of good moral character, having lived in an adulterous relationship with one man while still married to another. However, the Board of Immigration Appeals in Washington, D.C. later sustained her appeal on March 25, 1956, after

---

"In the Matter of Ngim Ah Oy on Habeas Corpus," Folder 23099R, Admiralty Files, U.S. District Court–San Francisco, RG 21, NARA-SF; and Alien File A6824153, obtained via Freedom of Information Act request to the Immigration and Naturalization Service.

her attorney cleverly argued that she had immigrated legally as a war
bride since her marriage to a citizen veteran had been consummated and
deemed valid by the immigration officer. Lee Puey You became a natu-
ralized U.S. citizen in 1959, which paved the way for her to send for her
family in China.

I was born in Cr 5-5-3 [June 3, 1916]. My name was Lee Puey You at
birth. When I was about 13 years old my father died and he did not leave
us anything and my family was very poor. It was during the war and my
family was having a hard time to make a living. One day a cousin of Woo
Tong talked to my mother and told her that he has a cousin in the United
States whose wife died recently and that he would like to remarry again
and asked my mother whether she was willing to consent to having
her daughter marry his cousin in the United States. Later Woo Tong's
cousin tell my mother to have a photograph of me to send it to Woo Tong
to see whether he liked me or not. Some time later Woo Tong's cousin
came and told me that I was to go to the United States under the name
of Ngin Ah Oy as a daughter of a son of a native—I was known as Yim
Tai Muey at that time—and that after I came to the United States I was
to marry Woo Tong as his wife, and I came to the United States in 1939.
When I arrived here in San Francisco, I was detained at Angel Island for
almost two years. During all of that time I had a very hard time and I was
very sad, and every time that someone was released from there I felt
sick all over again. I did not know what was happening to my case. I even
attempted suicide. Then later I was deported back to Hong Kong. On
my way back to Hong Kong I wanted to commit suicide again, but I was
thinking about my mother, of the hard times we had together. When I
arrived back in Hong Kong, I sold rice on the street in Hong Kong. I was
having a very hard time because it was during the war at that time. My
mother told me that we have used some of Woo Tong's money and no
matter how hard a time I am having I must not get married. She already
promised my marriage to Woo Tong. She said that I should wait until
after the war, when she could correspond with Woo Tong again and that
he will make arrangements for me to go to the United States again. After
the war, in about 1947, Woo Tong came to Hong Kong and he came to our
house and talked to my mother. Later then, we invited some friends for
dinner; then my mother told me it was considered as my marriage cere-
mony with Woo Tong. Then Woo Tong told me of his plan to bring me to
the United States. He said I was to get a marriage certificate with Nam
Chan and said I was to come to the United States as Nam Chan's wife and

said he would accompany me to the United States. After Nam Chan and I obtained our marriage certificate from the American Consular Office in Hong Kong, he told me that I must go to a husband and wife relationship with him before he could bring me to the United States. I objected to that, but he forced me into that, so I lived with him as man and wife in Hong Kong. Nam Chan and I came to the United States together in 1947. After we arrived in the United States, he took me to Woo Tong's place at 1141 Stockton Street and he left me there. When I get there I learned Woo Tong's wife was still living and that I was not actually to be Woo Tong's wife, but his concubine. I objected to it, but there was nothing I could do because I was new here in the United States. I did not know of anyone to go to for aid, so I stayed with him. During all those times I was living there I was treated very badly by his wife. She treated me as a slave girl. I had to do all kinds of work in the house, take care of her and I also had to take care of one of Woo Tong's buildings. On January 8, 1949 I gave birth to a daughter fathered by Woo Tong. While I was in the Stanford Hospital during my maternity period, Woo Tong made all the arrangements for me. He filled out the birth certificate for my daughter and he filled out the father's name as Nam Chan. Woo Tong died August 18, 1950 in San Francisco. After he died, his wife forced me to continue to work for her. When Woo Tong died, he did not leave money or anything for my daughter and myself. . . .

I met Fred Gin in about 1953 and learned his wife had passed away several years before. I found he was a person of good character. I went with him about six months before we got married. I went to Reno and obtained a divorce decree from Nam Chan to clear the record on January 16, 1953. Fred Gin had two sons by his first wife in the United States and after we were married, I bore him a daughter on February 4, 1955.

27

A Chinese Poem Left by a Deportee

*The ordeal of immigration and incarceration left an indelible mark in
the minds of many Chinese, a number of whom wrote poetry on the barracks' walls, recording their voyages to America, their longing for families
back home, and the outrage and humiliation they felt at their mistreatment. Many of the poems were originally written in pencil or ink. But
as immigration officials repeatedly ordered the walls repainted to cover
up what they considered graffiti, the poets began carving the outlines of
the Chinese calligraphy with a knife to create impressions of each word.
Maintenance crews began to fill in the wood with putty before applying
new coats of paint over them. Although the putty and paint succeeded in
obliterating many of the carved poems, they also served as sealers that
helped preserve the wood from further deterioration. Over the years,
the putty shrank and the different layers of paint cracked, revealing the
carved poems underneath.*

*Often haunting and poignant in their directness and simplicity of
language, the poems express a vitality and spirit of indomitability never
before identified with Chinese America. They chronicle the indignity and
trauma suffered at the hands of racist immigration systems, while con-
veying a spirit of resistance, perseverance, and Chinese nationalism in
the face of adversity. A few are farewell verses written by deportees, while
others are accounts of tribulations by transients bound to or from Mexico
and Cuba. This well-preserved poem was found in the lavatory on the first
floor of the detention barracks. It was written in two stanzas with four
vertical lines per stanza and seven characters per line; lines were written
to be read from left to right.*

"Poem 135," Him Mark Lai, Genny Lim, and Judy Yung, from *Island: Poetry and History
of Chinese Immigrants on Angel Island, 1910–1940*, 2nd ed. (Seattle: University of
Washington Press, 2014), 162.

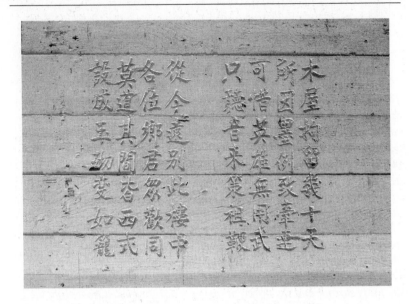

Photograph by Mak Takahashi.
Courtesy of Philip P. Choy Collection.

Detained in this wooden house for several tens of days,
It is all because of the Mexican exclusion law[1] which implicates me.
It's a pity heroes have no way of exercising their prowess.
I can only await the word so that I can snap Zu's whip.[2]

From now on, I am departing far from this building.
All of my fellow villagers are rejoicing with me.
Don't say that everything within is Western styled.
Even if it is built of jade, it has turned into a cage.

[1]In 1921, the Mexican government revised its treaty with China to ban the immigration of Chinese laborers, and in 1931, an expulsion order forced hundreds of Chinese Mexicans to leave their homes in Sonora and Sinaloa and cross the border into the United States. Many were detained on Angel Island while waiting to be deported to China.

[2]Zu Ti (266–321) was a general during the Western Jin dynasty (256–316). When non-Chinese people seized control of the Yellow River Valley in the fourth century and the Chinese court had to retreat to the south, Zu Ti swore to recover the lost territory. One of his friends, also a general, once said, "I sleep with my weapon awaiting the dawn. My ambition is to kill the barbarian enemy, but I am always afraid that Zu will crack the whip before me." Thus, the reference means to try hard and compete to be first.

4

Addressing a Historic Mistake

28

PRESIDENT FRANKLIN D. ROOSEVELT

Message to Congress on Repeal of the Chinese Exclusion Laws

October 11, 1943

World War II proved to be a watershed for Asian Americans after the United States became allies with China following the Japanese attack on Pearl Harbor. Over 120,000 Japanese Americans on the West Coast were stripped of their civil rights and herded into internment camps for the duration of the war. In contrast, President Franklin D. Roosevelt, in an effort to boost Chinese morale on the Pacific front as well as counter Japanese propaganda about U.S. imperialism and anti-Asian racism, urged Congress to pass the Magnuson bill, which would repeal the thirteen Chinese exclusion laws passed between 1882 and 1913, allow Chinese immigration at the nominal rate of 105 persons annually, and grant naturalization rights to Chinese residents. Although there was still opposition in Congress and from labor, veteran, and patriotic organizations that regarded Chinese immigration as an economic and racial threat to the nation, repeal was broadly supported by Democrats and Republicans in both chambers, thanks to the lobbying efforts of the Citizens' Committee to Repeal Chinese Exclusion, a powerful group of

"Text of Roosevelt's Plea to Repeal Exclusion Act," *San Francisco Chronicle*, October 12, 1943, 4; and 89 *Congressional Record* 8576 (1943).

white American friends of China led by New York publisher Richard Walsh. The Magnuson bill passed by voice vote on December 8, 1943, and was signed into law by President Roosevelt on December 17, 1943.

There is now pending before the Congress legislation to permit the immigration of Chinese people into this country and to allow Chinese residents here to become American citizens. I regard this legislation as important in the cause of winning the war and establishing a secure peace.

China is our ally. For many long years she stood alone in the fight against aggression. Today we fight at her side. She has continued her gallant struggle against very great odds.

China has understood that the strategy of victory in this World War first required the concentration of the greater part of our strength upon the European front. She has understood that the amount of supplies we could make available to her has been limited by difficulties of transportation. She knows that substantial aid will be forthcoming as soon as possible—aid not only in the form of weapons and supplies, but also in carrying out plans already made for offensive, effective actions. We and our Allies will aim our forces at the heart of Japan—in ever-increasing strength until the common enemy is driven from China's soil.

But China's resistance does not depend alone on guns and planes and on attacks on land, on the sea, and from the air. It is based as much in the spirit of her people and her faith in her Allies. We owe it to the Chinese to strengthen that faith. One step in this direction is to wipe from the statute books those anachronisms in our laws which forbid the immigration of Chinese people into this country and which bars Chinese residents from American citizenship.

Nations like individuals make mistakes. We must be big enough to acknowledge our mistakes of the past and to correct them.

By the repeal of the Chinese exclusion laws, we can correct a historic mistake and silence the distorted Japanese propaganda. The enactment of legislation now pending before the Congress would put Chinese immigrants on a parity with those from other countries. The Chinese quota would therefore be only about 100 immigrants a year. There can be no reasonable apprehension that any such number of immigrants will cause unemployment or provide competition in the search for jobs.

The extension of the privileges of citizenship to the relatively few Chinese residents in our country would operate as another meaningful display of friendship. It would be additional proof that we regard China not only as a partner in waging war but that we shall regard her as a partner in days of peace. While it would give the Chinese a preferred status over certain other Oriental people, their great contribution to the cause of decency and freedom entitles them to such preference.

I feel confident that the Congress is in full agreement that these measures—long overdue—should be taken to correct an injustice to our friends. Action by the Congress now will be an earnest endeavor of our purpose to apply the policy of the good neighbor to our relations with other peoples.

29

Senate Resolution 201
May 26, 2011

In 2010, close to the 130th anniversary of the Chinese Exclusion Act, Ted Gong of the Chinese American Citizens Alliance and Haipei Hsu of the National Council of Chinese Americans both felt it was time to lobby Congress to redress the exclusion laws and broaden public awareness of their history, harm, and injustice. To this end, they cofounded the 1882 Project and sought the pro bono support of Martin Gold and Covington and Burling LLP. In one year's time, the 1882 Project was able to mobilize grassroots support and secure commitments from Representatives Judy Chu (D-CA) and Judy Biggert (R-IL) and Senators Scott Brown (R-MA) and Dianne Feinstein (D-CA) to introduce legislation that they helped to draft. To ensure bipartisan and unanimous approval in both houses, the steering committee agreed to control three controversial issues. There was to be no mention of financial reparations (thus the resolution was to be an expression of regret rather than an apology), contemporary immigration reform, and U.S.–China bilateral rivalry. Senate Resolution 201 moved quickly and passed unanimously on October 6, 2011. The House Resolution, however, had to be redrafted to suit a more conservative body of representatives. House Resolution 683 was approved by voice vote without any objections on June 18, 2012. The success speaks to the political empowerment of Asian Americans made possible by the liberalization of immigration laws and civil rights since the 1960s.

Senate Resolution 201, 112th Congress, 57 *Congressional Record* S6352-54, October 6, 2011.

112TH CONGRESS, 1ST SESSION, S. RES. 201: Expressing the regret of the Senate for the passage of discriminatory laws against the Chinese in America, including the Chinese Exclusion Act.

IN THE SENATE OF THE UNITED STATES
MAY 26, 2011

Mr. BROWN of Massachusetts (for himself, Mrs. FEINSTEIN, Mr. HATCH, Mrs. MURRAY, Mr. CARDIN, Mr. RUBIO, Mr. AKAKA, Mr. KIRK, Mr. CARPER, Mr. COONS, and Mr. HOEVEN) submitted the following resolution; which was referred to the Committee on the Judiciary

OCTOBER 6, 2011

Committee discharged; considered, amended, and agreed to

RESOLUTION

Expressing the regret of the Senate for the passage of discriminatory laws against the Chinese in America, including the Chinese Exclusion Act.

Whereas many Chinese came to the United States in the 19th and 20th centuries, as did people from other countries, in search of the opportunity to create a better life for themselves and their families;

Whereas the contributions of persons of Chinese descent in the agriculture, mining, manufacturing, construction, fishing, and canning industries were critical to establishing the foundations for economic growth in the Nation, particularly in the western United States;

Whereas United States industrialists recruited thousands of Chinese workers to assist in the construction of the Nation's first major national transportation infrastructure, the Transcontinental Railroad;

Whereas Chinese laborers, who made up the majority of the western portion of the railroad workforce, faced grueling hours and extremely harsh conditions in order to lay hundreds of miles of track and were paid substandard wages;

Whereas without the tremendous efforts and technical contributions of these Chinese immigrants, the completion of this vital national infrastructure would have been seriously impeded;

Whereas from the middle of the 19th century through the early 20th century, Chinese immigrants faced racial ostracism and violent assaults, including—

(1) the 1887 Snake River Massacre in Oregon, at which 31 Chinese miners were killed; and

(2) numerous other incidents, including attacks on Chinese immigrants in Rock Springs, San Francisco, Tacoma, and Los Angeles;

Whereas the United States instigated the negotiation of the Burlingame Treaty, ratified by the Senate on October 19, 1868, which permitted the free movement of the Chinese people to, from, and within the United States and accorded to China the status of "most favored nation";

Whereas before consenting to the ratification of the Burlingame Treaty, the Senate required that the Treaty would not permit Chinese immigrants in the United States to be naturalized United States citizens;

Whereas on July 14, 1870, Congress approved An Act to Amend the Naturalization Laws and to Punish Crimes against the Same, and for other Purposes, and during consideration of such Act, the Senate expressly rejected an amendment to allow Chinese immigrants to naturalize;

Whereas Chinese immigrants were subject to the overzealous implementation of the Page Act of 1875 (18 Stat. 477), which—

(1) ostensibly barred the importation of women from "China, Japan, or any Oriental country" for purposes of prostitution;

(2) was disproportionately enforced against Chinese women, effectively preventing the formation of Chinese families in the United States and limiting the number of native-born Chinese citizens;

Whereas, on February 15, 1879, the Senate passed "the Fifteen Passenger Bill," which would have limited the number of Chinese passengers permitted on any ship coming to the United States to 15, with proponents of the bill expressing that the Chinese were "an indigestible element in our midst . . . without any adaptability to become citizens";

Whereas, on March 1, 1879, President Hayes vetoed the Fifteen Passenger Bill as being incompatible with the Burlingame Treaty, which declared that "Chinese subjects visiting or residing in the United States, shall enjoy the same privileges . . . in respect to travel or residence, as may there be enjoyed by the citizens and subjects of the most favored nation";

Whereas in the aftermath of the veto of the Fifteen Passenger Bill, President Hayes initiated the renegotiation of the Burlingame Treaty, requesting that the Chinese government consent to restrictions on the immigration of Chinese persons to the United States;

Whereas these negotiations culminated in the Angell Treaty, ratified by the Senate on May 9, 1881, which—

(1) allowed the United States to suspend, but not to prohibit, the immigration of Chinese laborers;

(2) declared that "Chinese laborers who are now in the United States shall be allowed to go and come of their own free will"; and

(3) reaffirmed that Chinese persons possessed "all the rights, privileges, immunities, and exemptions which are accorded to the citizens and subjects of the most favored nation";

Whereas, on March 9, 1882, the Senate passed the first Chinese Exclusion Act, which purported to implement the Angell Treaty but instead excluded for 20 years both skilled and unskilled Chinese laborers, rejected an amendment that would have permitted the naturalization of Chinese persons, and instead expressly denied Chinese persons the right to be naturalized as American citizens;

Whereas, on April 4, 1882, President Chester A. Arthur vetoed the first Chinese Exclusion Act as being incompatible with the terms and spirit of the Angell Treaty;

Whereas, on May 6, 1882, Congress passed the second Chinese Exclusion Act, which —

(1) prohibited skilled and unskilled Chinese laborers from entering the United States for 10 years;

(2) was the first Federal law that excluded a single group of people on the basis of race; and

(3) required certain Chinese laborers already legally present in the United States who later wished to reenter to obtain "certificates of return", an unprecedented requirement that applied only to Chinese residents;

Whereas in response to reports that courts were bestowing United States citizenship on persons of Chinese descent, the Chinese Exclusion Act of 1882 explicitly prohibited all State and Federal courts from naturalizing Chinese persons;

Whereas the Chinese Exclusion Act of 1882 underscored the belief of some Senators at that time that —

(1) the Chinese people were unfit to be naturalized;

(2) the social characteristics of the Chinese were "revolting";

(3) Chinese immigrants were "like parasites"; and

(4) the United States "is under God a country of Caucasians, a country of white men, a country to be governed by white men";

Whereas, on July 3, 1884, notwithstanding United States treaty obligations with China and other nations, Congress broadened the scope of the Chinese Exclusion Act —

(1) to apply to all persons of Chinese descent, "whether subjects of China or any other foreign power"; and

(2) to provide more stringent requirements restricting Chinese immigration;

Whereas, on October 1, 1888, the Scott Act was enacted into law, which —

(1) prohibited all Chinese laborers who would choose or had chosen to leave the United States from reentering;

(2) cancelled all previously issued "certificates of return", which prevented approximately 20,000 Chinese laborers abroad, including 600 individuals who were en route to the United States, from returning to their families or their homes; and

(3) was later determined by the Supreme Court to have abrogated the Angell Treaty;

Whereas, on May 5, 1892, the Geary Act was enacted into law, which—

(1) extended the Chinese Exclusion Act for 10 years;

(2) required all Chinese persons in the United States, but no other race of people, to register with the Federal Government in order to obtain "certificates of residence"; and

(3) denied Chinese immigrants the right to be released on bail upon application for a writ of habeas corpus;

Whereas on an explicitly racial basis, the Geary Act deemed the testimony of Chinese persons, including American citizens of Chinese descent, per se insufficient to establish the residency of a Chinese person subject to deportation, mandating that such residence be established through the testimony of "at least one credible white witness";

Whereas in the 1894 Gresham-Yang Treaty, the Chinese government consented to a prohibition of Chinese immigration and the enforcement of the Geary Act in exchange for the readmission of previous Chinese residents;

Whereas in 1898, the United States—

(1) annexed Hawaii;

(2) took control of the Philippines; and

(3) excluded thousands of racially Chinese residents of Hawaii and of the Philippines from entering the United States mainland;

Whereas on April 29, 1902, Congress—

(1) indefinitely extended all laws regulating and restricting Chinese immigration and residence; and

(2) expressly applied such laws to United States insular territories, including the Philippines;

Whereas in 1904, after the Chinese government exercised its unilateral right to withdraw from the Gresham-Yang Treaty, Congress permanently extended, "without modification, limitation, or condition", all restrictions on Chinese immigration and naturalization, making the Chinese the only racial group explicitly singled out for immigration exclusion and permanently ineligible for American citizenship;

Whereas between 1910 and 1940, the Angel Island Immigration Station implemented the Chinese exclusion laws by—

(1) confining Chinese persons for up to nearly 2 years;

(2) interrogating Chinese persons; and

(3) providing a model for similar immigration stations at other locations on the Pacific coast and in Hawaii;

Whereas each of the congressional debates concerning issues of Chinese civil rights, naturalization, and immigration involved intensely racial rhetoric, with many Members of Congress claiming that all persons of Chinese descent were—

(1) unworthy of American citizenship;

(2) incapable of assimilation into American society; and

(3) dangerous to the political and social integrity of the United States;

Whereas the express discrimination in these Federal statutes politically and racially stigmatized Chinese immigration into the United States, enshrining in law the exclusion of the Chinese from the political process and the promise of American freedom;

Whereas wartime enemy forces used the anti-Chinese legislation passed in Congress as evidence of American racism against the Chinese, attempting to undermine the Chinese-American alliance and allied military efforts;

Whereas, in 1943, at the urging of President Franklin D. Roosevelt, and over 60 years after the enactment of the first discriminatory laws against Chinese immigrants, Congress—

(1) repealed previously enacted anti-Chinese legislation; and

(2) permitted Chinese immigrants to become naturalized United States citizens;

Whereas despite facing decades of systematic, pervasive, and sustained discrimination, Chinese immigrants and Chinese-Americans persevered and have continued to play a significant role in the growth and success of the United States;

Whereas 6 decades of Federal legislation deliberately targeting Chinese by race—

(1) restricted the capacity of generations of individuals and families to openly pursue the American dream without fear; and

(2) fostered an atmosphere of racial discrimination that deeply prejudiced the civil rights of Chinese immigrants;

Whereas diversity is one of our Nation's greatest strengths, and, while this Nation was founded on the principle that all persons are created equal, the laws enacted by Congress in the late 19th and early 20th centuries that restricted the political and civil rights of persons of Chinese descent violated that principle;

Whereas although an acknowledgment of the Senate's actions that contributed to discrimination against persons of Chinese descent will not erase the past, such an expression will acknowledge and illuminate the injustices in our national experience and help to build a better and stronger Nation;

Whereas the Senate recognizes the importance of addressing this unique framework of discriminatory laws in order to educate the public and future generations regarding the impact of these laws on Chinese and other Asian persons and their implications to all Americans; and

Whereas the Senate deeply regrets the enactment of the Chinese Exclusion Act and related discriminatory laws that—

(1) resulted in the persecution and political alienation of persons of Chinese descent;

(2) unfairly limited their civil rights;

(3) legitimized racial discrimination; and

(4) induced trauma that persists within the Chinese community: Now, therefore, be it

Resolved,

SECTION 1. ACKNOWLEDGMENT AND EXPRESSION OF REGRET.

The Senate—

(1) acknowledges that this framework of anti-Chinese legislation, including the Chinese Exclusion Act, is incompatible with the basic founding principles recognized in the Declaration of Independence that all persons are created equal;

(2) deeply regrets passing 6 decades of legislation directly targeting the Chinese people for physical and political exclusion and the wrongs committed against Chinese and American citizens of Chinese descent who suffered under these discriminatory laws; and

(3) reaffirms its commitment to preserving the same civil rights and constitutional protections for people of Chinese or other Asian descent in the United States accorded to all others, regardless of their race or ethnicity.

SECTION 2. DISCLAIMER.

Nothing in this resolution may be construed—

(1) to authorize or support any claim against the United States; or

(2) to serve as a settlement of any claim against the United States.

A Chronology of Chinese Immigration and Exclusion (1784–2012)

1784 U.S.–China trade begins with the voyage of the *Empress of China* from New York to Canton.

1790 Congress passes Naturalization Act limiting naturalization to "free White persons of good character."

1808 Congress prohibits Americans from participating in African slave trade.

1839–1842 China is defeated in Opium War against Britain and forced to sign Treaty of Nanking, opening five ports to trade, ceding Hong Kong to Britain, and granting extraterritorial rights to foreigners.

1844 Treaty of Wangxia gives the United States most favored nation status in trade and extraterritorial rights in China.

1848 Gold is discovered at John Sutter's Sawmill, north of San Francisco, sparking the California Gold Rush and Chinese immigration to the United States.

1850–1864 Taiping Rebellion against the Qing dynasty (1644–1911) sweeps through Central and South China.

1851 California is admitted into the Union as a free state.

1852 Hawaiian plantation owners import 195 Chinese contract laborers; over 20,000 Chinese migrants arrive in California for the Gold Rush; Foreign Miners' Tax of $4 a month is mainly imposed on Chinese miners.

1854 In *People v. Hall,* California Supreme Court rules that no Chinese person can testify against a white person in court. The ruling stands until 1873.

1855 California imposes $50 Capitation Tax on ship masters for every Chinese passenger they transport to a California port.

1860   Britain and France defeat China in Second Opium War; Treaty of
             Tientsin opens more ports, legalizes opium, and cedes Kowloon
             to Britain.

1861–
1865   Civil War is fought over the expansion of slavery into the western
             states; over 70 Chinese fought on both sides of the war.

1862   U.S. government prohibits coolie trade by American vessels.

1863–
1869   12,000 Chinese railroad workers are hired by the Central Pacific
             Railroad Company to build the western section of the transconti-
             nental railroad.

1865   Thirteenth Amendment prohibiting slavery is ratified.

1868   Burlingame Treaty between the United States and China permits
             free and voluntary immigration from China and grants Chinese
             same treatment accorded to citizens of most favored nations; Four-
             teenth Amendment is ratified, establishing citizenship rights for all
             persons born or naturalized in the United States.

1870   Naturalization Act of 1870 limits naturalization to persons of Afri-
             can descent and to whites. An amendment to extend naturaliza-
             tion rights to Chinese persons is defeated.

1871   Chinese residents in Los Angeles Chinatown are attacked,
             robbed, and killed by a mob of white men 500 strong; 17 Chinese
             are lynched.

1873   Discriminatory ordinances like the Queue Ordinance and Laun-
             dry Ordinance are passed in San Francisco to harass and drive
             Chinese workers away.

1875   Page Law bars importation of Chinese and Japanese prosti-
             tutes, felons, and contract laborers; In *Chy Lung v. Freeman,*
             U.S. Supreme Court declares that control over immigration is a
             federal responsibility and that state efforts are unconstitutional;
             Civil Rights Act enacted to protect the equal rights of all citizens
             in public accommodation, transportation, and jury service.

1876   California State Senate appoints bipartisan committee to hold
             hearings and investigate the "evils of Chinese immigration";
             Congress appoints and sends Joint Special Committee to the
             West Coast to do likewise.

1877   The Panic of 1877 throws millions out of work; Workingmen's
             Party of California founded under the leadership of Denis
             Kearney; three-day anti-Chinese riot in San Francisco results in
             the looting and torching of fifteen laundries, four deaths, and
             fourteen wounded.

1879   California Constitution prohibits corporations and public works from hiring Chinese, voids all contracts for coolie labor, allows for the removal of Chinese from cities and towns, and discourages their immigration by all means; Congress passes Fifteen Passenger Bill, but it is vetoed by President Rutherford B. Hayes.

1880   China and the United States sign the Angell Treaty, which permits the United States to restrict or suspend, but not prohibit immigration of Chinese laborers; California prohibits marriage between whites and "Mongolians, Negroes, mulattoes, and persons of mixed blood"; this law stands until ruled unconstitutional by the California Supreme Court in 1948 and by the U.S. Supreme Court in 1967.

1882   President Chester A. Arthur signs the Chinese Exclusion Act into law on May 6, suspending immigration of Chinese laborers for ten years and denying naturalization rights to Chinese persons.

1885   Chinese miners are massacred in Rock Springs, Wyoming; Alien Contract Labor Law applies to all Chinese laborers seeking to enter the United States from anyplace in the world.

1886   In *Yick Wo v. Hopkins*, the U.S. Supreme Court invokes the Equal Protection Clause of the Fourteenth Amendment to protect Chinese laundry owners against discriminatory ordinances.

1888   United States and China negotiate Bayard-Zhang Treaty, which allows the United States to prohibit immigration of Chinese laborers, but China refuses to ratify the treaty; Congress passes Scott Act, rendering 20,000 Chinese reentry certificates null and void.

1892   Geary Law extends exclusion policy for ten years and requires Chinese to register and carry papers proving their right to be in the United States or face immediate deportation; Ellis Island opens in New York as the gateway to America for 12 million European immigrants until it closes in 1954.

1893   *Fong Yue Ting v. U.S.* upholds constitutionality of Geary Law; Congress passes McCreary Amendment to extend the deadline for Chinese to register by six months.

1894   China and the United States ratify the Gresham-Yang Treaty allowing the United States to prohibit immigration of Chinese laborers; Pullman Strike over wages shuts down nation's freight and passenger traffic west of Detroit, Michigan, resulting in violence breaking out in many cities.

1898   In *Wong Kim Ark v. U.S.,* the U.S. Supreme Court rules that a Chinese person born in the United States cannot be stripped of his citizenship; Spanish-American War cedes Puerto Rico, Guam, and the Philippines to the United States; Congress extends Chinese exclusion laws to cover annexed Hawaii; Pacific Mail Steamship Company converts offices at Pier 40 into a detention shed.

1902   Chinese Exclusion Act is extended indefinitely and made applicable to U.S. insular possessions, including the Philippines.

1904   China renounces the Gresham-Yang Treaty; Chinese Exclusion Act is extended permanently.

1905   Shanghai merchants organize a ten month boycott of American imports in China to protest mistreatment of Chinese immigrants in the United States; *Ju Toy v. United States* decision stops Chinese immigrants from appealing their cases to the higher courts.

1906   Earthquake and fire in San Francisco destroys birth records and facilitates the entry of Chinese immigrants as "paper sons" claiming derivative citizenship.

1907–1908   Under the Gentlemen's Agreement, Japan agrees to prohibit emigration of Japanese laborers to the United States.

1910–1940   Angel Island Immigration Station opens in 1910 and shuts down in 1940 after a fire destroys the administration building.

1911   Sun Yat-sen's Revolutionary Army succeeds in overthrowing the Qing dynasty and establishing the Republic of China.

1913   California passes Alien Land Act prohibiting an "alien ineligible to citizenship"—a legal classification that applied only to Asians—from buying land; declared unconstitutional by the California Supreme Court in 1952.

1914–1918   United States enters World War I in 1917; all aliens, including Chinese, who served in the war are entitled to U.S. citizenship.

1917   Immigration Act of 1917 prohibits immigration from the Asiatic Barred Zone, which includes India, Burma, Siam, the Malay States, Arabia, Afghanistan, part of Russia, and most of the Polynesian Islands.

1922   Cable Act stipulates that any female citizen who marries an alien ineligible for citizenship loses her U.S. citizenship; amended and repealed in 1931.

1924   Immigration Act of 1924 restricts immigration from Southern and Eastern European countries based on a national origin quota system and bars immigration of all aliens ineligible to citizenship, including Japanese.

1937   Japan invades China, sparking the Sino-Japanese War, which lasts until 1945.

1941   Japan attacks Pearl Harbor and the United States enters World War II as China's ally; 15,000 Chinese Americans enlist in the armed services and earn U.S. citizenship; 120,000 Japanese Americans become "enemy aliens" and are removed from the West Coast and locked up in internment camps for the duration of the war.

1943   The Magnuson Act repeals the Chinese exclusion laws, establishes an annual quota of 105 Chinese immigrants, and allows Chinese to become naturalized citizens.

1945   World War II ends after the United States drop atomic bombs on Hiroshima and Nagasaki; War Brides Act allows immigration of Asian wives of U.S. servicemen between 1946 and 1953.

1946   Congress passes the Luce-Celler Bill to establish annual quotas of 100 for immigrants from India and the Philippines and to grant them naturalization rights.

1949   Chinese Communist leader Mao Zedong establishes the People's Republic of China, and the United States breaks diplomatic relations with China.

1952   Intended to protect the nation against Communist infiltration and subversion, the McCarran-Walter Act upholds the national origins quota system, allots each Asian country a minimum of one hundred visas annually, and extends naturalization rights to all Asian groups.

1956   INS establishes Confession Program to go after Communist sympathizers and end the paper son practice by offering illegal immigrants the opportunity to confess and clear their names.

1964   Congress passes Civil Rights Act to prohibit discrimination in education, employment, and public accommodations on the basis of race, sex, religion, or national origin.

1965   Congress passes Voting Rights Act to prohibit discriminatory voting practices; and Immigration and Nationality Act, replacing the racist quotas of the Immigration Act of 1924 with equal quotas for all countries and giving preference to family reunification.

1979   The United States reestablishes diplomatic ties with China, and direct immigration from China to the United States resumes.

2012   Congress unanimously passes resolutions of regret for the Chinese exclusion laws.

Questions for Consideration

1. What were the socioeconomic and political causes behind the Chinese Exclusion Act of 1882 (Documents 1–15)?

2. How and why was the treatment of European immigrants at Ellis Island different from that of Chinese immigrants at Angel Island (Documents 21–27)?

3. How would you have argued for or against Chinese exclusion as a white laborer, capitalist, missionary, hardline Democrat, liberal Republican, or Chinese immigrant (Documents 1–7)?

4. What were the main arguments for and against Chinese exclusion in Congress (Documents 6–7)? Why did those in favor of exclusion win?

5. How do you see the debate over Chinese exclusion as illuminating or complicating the American conversation about slavery, race, and citizenship (Documents 1–7)?

6. How did media perceptions and stereotypes of Chinese men and women influence immigration policy in the late nineteenth century (Documents 8–15)? How does this compare to that of Mexican men and women in the twenty-first century?

7. How did Chinese immigrants resist exclusion in the nineteenth century (Documents 2, 4, 18–27)? How does this compare to targeted immigrant groups today?

8. What strategies were employed by Chinese immigrants to gain entry into the United States, and how did the immigration service thwart their efforts (Documents 16–27)? How could the Chinese exclusion laws have been better enforced?

9. Based on her immigration file and story, did Lee Puey You deserve to be excluded and deported (Documents 24–26)? Why or why not?

10. How did race, class, gender, and nationality affect the experience of Chinese men and women on Angel Island (Documents 21–27)?

11. Given that immigrant detention has become the fastest growing form of incarceration in the United States, how do the numbers and conditions of detention today compare with that of Angel Island during the time of Chinese exclusion? (Documents 23–26)?

12. How effective was Chinese poetry as a means of resistance and expression for detainees at Angel Island (Documents 23, 24, 27)? What medium would you choose and what message would you leave if you found yourself in a similar situation?

13. Do you agree with the arguments for repeal in 1943 and regrets in 2011 (Documents 28 and 29)? Why or why not?

14. How was Chinese illegal immigration resolved after F.D.R.'s *Message to Congress* (Document 28)? Does this shed light onto how we should deal with the large population of undocumented immigrants today?

15. What elements make for an effective but fair immigration policy according to our Constitutional values? Given your answer, how would you reform U.S. immigration policy?

Selected Bibliography

BOOKS AND ARTICLES

Architectural Resources Group and Daniel Quan Design. "Poetry and Inscriptions: Translation and Analysis." Prepared by Charles Egan, Wan Liu, Newton Liu, and Xing Chu Wang for the California Department of Parks and Recreation and Angel Island Immigration Station Foundation, San Francisco, 2004.

Barde, Robert. *Immigration at the Golden Gate: Passenger Ships, Exclusion, and Angel Island.* Westport, CT: Praeger, 2008.

Barth, Gunther. *Bitter Strength: A History of the Chinese in the United States, 1850–1870.* Cambridge, MA: Harvard University Press, 1964.

Becker, Jules. *The Course of Exclusion, 1882–1924: San Francisco Newspaper Coverage of the Chinese and Japanese in the United States.* San Francisco, CA: Mellen Research University Press, 1991.

Bolton, Joseph. "Cerebrospinal Meningitis at Angel Island Immigration Station, Calif." *Public Health Reports* 36, no. 12 (March 25, 1921): 593–602.

California State Senate Special Committee on Chinese Immigration. *Chinese Immigration: The Social, Moral and Political Effect.* Sacramento, CA: State Printing Office, 1877.

Camacho, Julia Maria Schiavone. *Chinese Mexicans: Transpacific Migration and a Search for a Homeland.* Chapel Hill: University of North Carolina Press, 2012.

Chan, Sucheng. *Asian Americans: An Interpretive History.* Woodbridge, CT: Twayne, 1991.

———, ed. *Chinese American Transnationalism: The Flow of People, Resources, and Ideas between China and America during the Exclusion Era.* Philadelphia, PA: Temple University Press, 2006.

———, ed. *Entry Denied: Exclusion and the Chinese Community in America, 1882–1943.* Philadelphia, PA: Temple University Press, 1991.

———. *This Bitter-sweet Soil: The Chinese in California Agriculture, 1860–1910.* Berkeley: University of California Press, 1986.

Chang, Iris. *The Chinese in America: A Narrative History.* New York: Viking, 2003.

Chen, Wen-hsien. "Chinese under Both Exclusion and Immigration Laws." PhD diss. University of Chicago, 1940.

Cheng, Lucie and Edna Bonacich, eds. *Labor Immigration under Capitalism: Asian Workers in the United States before World War II.* Berkeley: University of California Press, 1984.

Chin, Tung Pok and Winifred C. Chin. *Paper Son: One Man's Story.* Philadelphia, PA: Temple University Press, 2000.

Chinn, Thomas W., H. Mark Lai, and Philip P. Choy. *A History of the Chinese in California: A Syllabus.* San Francisco, CA: Chinese Historical Society of America, 1969.

Chiu, Ping. *Chinese Labor in California, 1850–1880: An Economic Study.* Madison: State Historical Society of Wisconsin, 1967.

Choy, Philip P., Lorraine Dong, and Marlon K. Hom. *The Coming Man: 19th Century Perceptions of the Chinese.* Hong Kong: Joint Publishing Company, 1994.

Chung, Sue Fawn. *In Pursuit of Gold: Chinese American Miners and Merchants in the American West.* Urbana: University of Illinois Press, 2011.

Coolidge, Mary Roberts. *Chinese Immigration.* New York: Henry Holt, 1909.

Delgado, Grace Pena. *Making the Chinese Mexican: Global Migration, Localism, and Exclusion in the U.S.–Mexican Borderlands.* Stanford, CA: Stanford University Press, 2012.

Gee, Jennifer. "Housewives, Men's Villages, and Sexual Respectability: Gender and the Interrogation of Asian Women at the Angel Island Immigration Station." In *Asian/Pacific Islander American Women: A Historical Anthology,* edited by Shirley Hune and Gail M. Nomura, 90–105. New York: New York University Press, 2003.

Gold, Martin B. *Forbidden Citizens: Chinese Exclusion and the U.S. Congress: A Legislative History.* Alexandria, VA: The Capitol Net, 2012.

Gyory, Andrew. *Closing the Gate: Race, Politics, and the Chinese Exclusion Act.* Chapel Hill: University of North Carolina Press, 1998.

Hing, Bill. *Making and Remaking Asian America through Immigration Policy.* Stanford, CA: Stanford University Press, 1993.

Hirata, Lucie Cheng. "Free, Indentured, Enslaved: Chinese Prostitutes in Nineteenth-Century America." *Signs: Journal of Women in Culture and Society* 5, no. 1 (Autumn 1979): 3–29.

Hoexter, Corinne K. *From Canton to California: The Epic of Chinese Immigration.* New York: Four Winds Press, 1976.

Hsu, Madeline. *Dreaming of Gold, Dreaming of Home: Transnationalism and Migration between the United States and South China, 1882–1943.* Stanford, CA: Stanford University Press, 2000.

Jorae, Wendy Rouse. *The Children of Chinatown: Growing Up Chinese American in San Francisco, 1850–1920.* Chapel Hill: University of North Carolina Press, 2009.

Lai, Him Mark. *Becoming Chinese American: A History of Communities and Institutions.* Walnut Creek, CA: Alta Mira Press, 2004.

Lai, Him Mark, Genny Lim, and Judy Yung. *Island: Poetry and History of Chinese Immigrants on Angel Island, 1910–1940,* 2nd edition. Seattle: University of Washington Press, 2014.

Lau, Estelle. *Paper Families: Identity, Immigration Administration, and Chinese Exclusion.* Durham, NC: Duke University Press, 2007.

Lee, Erika. *At America's Gates: Chinese Immigration during the Exclusion Era, 1882–1943.* Chapel Hill: University of North Carolina Press, 2003.

————. "Exclusion Acts: Chinese Women during the Chinese Exclusion Era, 1882–1943." In *Asian/Pacific Islander American Women: A Historical Anthology,* edited by Shirley Hune and Gail M. Nomura, 77–89. New York: New York University Press, 2003.

————. *The Making of Asian America: A History.* New York: Simon & Schuster, 2015.

Lee, Erika and Judy Yung. *Angel Island: Immigrant Gateway to America.* New York: Oxford University Press, 2010.

Lee, Moonbeam Tong. *Growing Up in Chinatown: The Life and Work of Edwar Lee.* 1987.

Lee, Robert. *Orientals: Asian Americans in Popular Culture.* Philadelphia, PA: Temple University Press, 1999.

McClellan, Robert. *The Heathen Chinee: A Study of American Attitudes toward China, 1890–1905.* Columbus: Ohio State University Press, 1971.

McClain, Charles J. *In Search of Equality: The Chinese Struggle against Discrimination in Nineteenth-Century America.* Berkeley: University of California Press, 1994.

McKee, Delber L. *Chinese Exclusion Versus the Open Door Policy, 1900–1906.* Detroit, MI: Wayne State University Press, 1977.

McKeown, Adam. "Ritualization of Regulation: The Enforcement of Chinese Exclusion in the United States and China." *American Historical Review* 108, no. 2 (April 2003): 377–403.

Miller, Stuart Creighton. *The Unwelcome Immigrant: The American Image of the Chinese, 1785–1882.* Berkeley: University of California Press, 1969.

Ngai, Mae M. "The Architecture of Race in American Immigration Law: A Reexamination of the Immigration Act of 1924." *Journal of American History* 86, no. 1 (June 1999): 80–88.

————. *Impossible Subjects: Illegal Aliens and the Making of Modern America.* Princeton, NJ: Princeton University Press, 2004.

————. "Legacies of Exclusion: Illegal Chinese Immigration during the Cold War Years." *Journal of American Ethnic History* 18, no. 1 (Fall 1998): 3–35.

————. *The Lucky Ones: One Family and the Extraordinary Invention of Chinese America.* Boston, MA: Houghton Mifflin Harcourt, 2010.

Peffer, George Anthony. *If They Don't Bring Their Women Here: Chinese Female Immigration before Exclusion.* Urbana: University of Illinois Press, 1999.

Pfaelzer, Jean. *Driven Out: The Forgotten War against Chinese Americans.* Berkeley: University of California Press, 2008.

The Repeal and Its Legacy: Proceedings of the Conference on the 50th Anniversary of the Repeal of the Exclusion Acts. San Francisco, CA: Chinese Historical Society of America and Asian American Studies, San Francisco State University, 1994.

Riggs, Fred. *Pressure on Congress: A Study of the Repeal of Chinese Exclusion.* New York: Columbia University Press, 1950.

Salyer, Lucy. *Laws Harsh as Tigers: Chinese Immigrants and the Shaping of Modern Immigration Law.* Chapel Hill: University of North Carolina Press, 1995.

Sabin, Edwin Legrand. *Building the Pacific Railway.* Philadelphia, PA: J. B. Lippincott, 1919.

Sandmeyer, Elmer Clarence. *The Anti-Chinese Movement in California.* Urbana: University of Illinois Press, 1973.

Saxton, Alexander. *The Indispensable Enemy: Labor and the Anti-Chinese Movement in California.* Berkeley: University of California Press, 1971.

Shah, Nayan. *Contagious Divides: Epidemics and Race in San Francisco Chinatown.* Berkeley: University of California Press, 2001.

Shen, I-yao. *A Century of Chinese Exclusion Abroad.* Beijing: Foreign Language Press, 2006.

Sinn, Elizabeth. *Pacific Crossing: California Gold, Chinese Migration, and the Making of Hong Kong.* Hong Kong: Hong Kong University Press, 2013.

Siu, Paul. *The Chinese Laundryman: A Study of Social Isolation.* New York: New York University Press, 1987.

Soennichsen, John. *Chinese Exclusion Act.* Santa Barbara, CA: Greenwood, 2011.

———. *Miwoks to Missiles: A History of Angel Island.* Tiburon, CA: Angel Island Association, 2005.

Takaki, Ronald. *A Different Mirror: A History of Multicultural America.* Boston, MA: Little, Brown and Company, 1993.

———. *Strangers from a Different Shore: A History of Asian Americans.* Boston, MA: Little, Brown and Company, 1989.

Tchen, John Kuo Wei. *New York before Chinatown: Orientalism and the Shaping of American Culture, 1776–1882.* Baltimore, MD: John Hopkins University Press, 1999.

Tchen, John Kuo Wei, and Dylan Yeats. *Yellow Peril: An Archive of Anti-Asian Fear.* London: Verso, 2014.

Tsai, Shih-shan Henry. *China and the Overseas Chinese in the United States, 1868–1911.* Fayetteville: University of Arkansas Press, 1983.

Tung, William L. *The Chinese in America, 1820–1973: A Chronology & Fact Book*. Dobbs Ferry, NY: Oceana, 1974.

U. S. Senate. Senate Report No. 689. *Report of the Joint Senate Committee to Investigate Chinese Immigration*. 44th Congress, 2nd session. Washington, DC: Government Printing Office, 1877.

Wong, K. Scott. *Americans First: Chinese Americans and the Second World War*. Cambridge, MA: Harvard University Press, 2005.

Wong, K. Scott, and Sucheng Chan, eds. *Claiming America: Constructing Chinese American Identities during the Exclusion Era*. Philadelphia, PA: Temple University Press, 1998.

Wong, Wayne Hung. *American Paper Son: A Chinese Immigrant in the Midwest*. Urbana: University of Illinois Press, 2006.

Yu, Connie Young. "Rediscovered Voices: Chinese Immigrants at Angel Island." *Amerasia Journal* 4, no. 2 (1977): 123–39.

Yu, Renqiu. *To Save China, To Save Ourselves: The Chinese Hand Laundry Alliance of New York*. Philadelphia, PA: Temple Univrsity Press, 1992.

Yung, Judy. *Unbound Feet: A Social History of Chinese Women in San Francisco*. Berkeley: University of California Press, 1995.

———. "Trump's Anti-Immigrant Campaign: Will We Repeat a Historic Mistake?" http://nomoreexclusion.org/unity-statement/, 2017.

Yung, Judy, Gordon H. Chang, and Him Mark Lai. *Chinese American Voices: From the Gold Rush to the Present*. Berkeley: University of California Press, 2006.

Zhao, Xiaojian. *Remaking Chinese America: Immigration, Family, and Community, 1940–1965*. New Brunswick, NJ: Rutgers University Press, 2002.

Zhu, Liping. *The Road to Chinese Exclusion: The Denver Riot, 1880 Election, and Rise of the West*. Lawrence: University Press of Kansas, 2013.

FILMS

Burns, Ric and Li-Shin Yu. *The Chinese Exclusion Act*. New York: Steeplechase Films, 2017.

Chen, Amy. *The Chinatown Files*. New York: Filmmakers Library, 2001.

Chen Zhuoling. *Roots Old and New: Stories of Chinese Emigrants, North America,* Episode 3—*No Angels on Angel Island*. Hong Kong: Radio Television Hong Kong (RTHK), 2012.

Lew, Jennie and Yvonne Lee, *Separate Lives, Broken Dreams*. San Francisco, CA: Center for Asian American Media, 1994.

Lowe, Felicia. *Carved in Silence*. San Francisco, CA: Felicia Lowe Productions, 1987.

———. *Chinese Couplets*. San Francisco, CA: Lowedown Productions, 2015.

Moyers, Bill. *Becoming Americans: The Chinese Experience*. Princeton, NJ: Films for the Humanities and Sciences, 2003.

Acknowledgments (*continued from p. ii*)

Document 21: Emery Sims, "Giving every applicant a square deal," 1929–1940. Emery Sims, interview with Judy Yung, Him Mark Lai, and Genny Lim, San Francisco, June 29, 1977. Interview #47, Angel Island Oral History Project, Ethnic Studies Library, University of California, Berkeley. Reprinted by permission.

Document 22: Edwar Lee, "Not a ghost of a chance for a Chinese to be an inspector," 1927–1938. Edwar Lee, interview with Him Mark Lai, Genny Lim, Judy Yung, and Nelson Yee, Oakland, CA, May 8, 1976; interview with Felicia Lowe, Oakland, CA, April 9, 1984. Interview #50, Angel Island Oral History Project, Ethnic Studies Library, University of California, Berkeley. Reprinted by permission.

Document 24: Lee Puey You, "A bowlful of tears," 1939–1940. Lee Puey You, interview with Him Mark Lai and Judy Yung, San Francisco, December 14, 1975, and interview with Felicia Lowe, San Francisco, April 11, 1984. Interview #11, Angel Island Oral History Project, Ethnic Studies Library, University of California, Berkeley. Reprinted by permission.

Document 27: A Chinese Poem Left by a Deportee. Poem 135, Him Mark Lai, Genny Lim, and Judy Yung, *Island: Poetry and History of Chinese Immigrants on Angel Island, 1910–1940,* 2nd ed. (Seattle: University of Washington Press, 2014), p. 162. Copyright © 1980 by the HOC DOI (History of Chinese Detained on Island) Project. Reprinted by permission.

Index

169